BEYOND THE

GRIDIRON

HOW TO SUCCESSFULLY TRANSITION

INTO COLLEGIATE FOOTBALL

SECOND EDITION

D1280283

TRAVIS B. KEY &
ASHTON HENDERSON

Travis B. Key & Ashton Henderson

Beyond the Gridiron: How to Successfully Transition into Collegiate Football

Copyright © 2017 by Travis Key and Ashton Henderson. All rights reserved.

No part of this publication may be reproduced, stored in a retrieval system or transmitted in any way by any means, electronic, mechanical, photocopy, recording or otherwise without the prior permission of the author except as provided by USA copyright law.

Scriptures taken from the Holy Bible, New International Version®, niv®. Copyright © 1973, 1978, 1984 by Biblica, Inc.™ Used by permission of Zondervan. All rights reserved worldwide. www.zondervan.com.

Published in the United States of America
ISBN-13: 978-1514863695
ISBN-10: 1514863693
1.   Sports & Recreation / Football
2.   Education / Student Life & Student Affairs

DEDICATIONS

To the most important people in my life—my mother (Jacqueline), my late grandmother (Eva), my late sister (Regina), and most importantly, my wife (Giovanna) and our two girls (Gianna and Malina) and son (Matteo). I hope I make you all proud!

— Travis

To everyone who has made an impact on my life, I am grateful and humbled for everything you have done for me. To my mother (Jacqueline), my father (Admiral), my brother (Antonio), my Godmother (Freddie) you inspired me to get this project completed, my Grandparents (Augustus and Geneva) thank you for being an example and most importantly, the love of my life and beautiful wife (Jasmyne). Thank you for inspiring us to write this book and always encouraging me to make this dream a reality.

— Ashton

CONTENTS

PREFACE

Being a collegiate athlete comes with a lot of pressure. More too often we see student athletes like you with a life of promise ahead of you, slipping and hitting the ground face first, awakened by the realities of these challenges (if you follow today's media, there are more than enough examples of this, so we will spare you of a long list of incidents). From the outside looking in, people often say, "what is wrong with kids these days," or "I can't believe he would make a dumb mistake like that and blow his entire career!" The reality is that you are a young person entering a multibillion dollar industry with very little knowledge about what it takes to be an adult, let alone a businessman. Most of you are physically and mentally unprepared for what you are about to encounter as a student-athlete.

Through our experience of being teammates, coaches, and administrators at the high school and collegiate levels, time and time again we have witnessed thousands of student-athletes just like you fail due to this lack of preparation. We have identified a huge void in our athletic system that is causing student-athletes with hopeful careers to continue to stumble their way out of competition on and off the field. Beyond the Gridiron: How to Successfully Transition into Collegiate Football has promised to turn the tide.

This book is structured to lay out a blueprint for you to follow as a student-athlete as you transition into and out of collegiate athletics. We provide insight on what it is going to take to rise above the pressure and position yourself for success on and off the field. We deliver firsthand knowledge and personal experiences throughout each chapter that all student-athletes can relate to and learn from. Our purpose is to equip incoming student-athletes with the tools to overcome, mental and physical challenges of collegiate athletics, and give each and every student-athlete who reads this book an honest shot at success.

THE JOURNEY

Ashton

Growing up in Tallahassee, Florida meant exposure to the game of football came at a young age. Having the Florida State Seminoles and the FAMU Rattlers in your backyard was something that every young kid in Tallahassee was extremely proud of. We all wanted to have the privilege of playing the game at that level.

According to my family, my love for the game started when I was still an infant. The majority of my baby pictures were taken in football gear or had some type of sports related theme. It seemed like everyone in my family knew that I had a strong affinity for the game of football and sports in general, but I had no idea that I would one day have the opportunity to play Division I football.

From time to time, many of my family members would share numerous stories with me regarding the passion I had for the game at such a young age. My late godfather always told me I was tough as a nail because when I hit my head I would get up like nothing ever happened. He also told me that I would always want to throw the ball with everyone, and I would throw a temper tantrum if the football was not in sight.

The most memorable moment my family shared with me was when my father had me doing push-ups at the age of two, and he would massage my calves every night before I went to bed. They have also told me my physique was not like an ordinary child, and that I was destined to be a football player. I embodied all the qualifying characteristics, and my father wanted to see if I would live up to the hype.

I can vividly remember my father registering me for the Tallahassee Parks and Recreation Flag Football league for six- to ten-year-olds. However, there was one problem, I was only five years old and was the youngest kid in the league. I was not the smallest kid, but I surely was not the biggest. Somehow I still managed to compete, and my dad called me lightening because I was very quick and I could elude defenders.

As time progressed, I began to gain confidence each week while I was playing with the older kids and it became pretty fun to run circles around our opponents. At that time, I did not realize I had a true gift. Unfortunately, one time I ran too many circles and ended up running to the opposite end zone for the other squad. My dad has that moment on VHS, and I am glad that he did not submit the footage to America's Funniest Home Videos because it would have been very embarrassing.

I really began to love football. I wanted to get better and critique everything I did at a young age. Both my parents supported me in all my endeavors, but football was very special to my father. He was a pretty good football player in high school, and most of his buddies spoke very highly of his athletic ability. His dreams of playing collegiate football were cut short due to a season-ending knee injury, which he still has problems with. I was charged to take the initiative to take my father's dream to play collegiate football and make him proud because he could live his dream through me.

I attended North Florida Christian School from grade school all the way up through tenth grade. My parents really wanted me to attend a private school to help establish a foundation academically as well as enhance my spiritual journey with God in an open setting. NFC was a very unique experience, and it helped me develop and grow into the person I am today. It also allowed me to play football at a very high level. In Tallahassee, there were two powerhouse schools for football: North Florida Christian and the juggernaut Lincoln High School. Both schools have a strong national presence and have produced quality

NFL players. Our football team at NFC was very good, and we were the preseason favorite to the win the state championship almost every year.

NFC had great academics, excellent sports programs, and most importantly for my family, it provided a space where I could talk freely about God. But for the many positive things they had to offer there was something missing, and I wanted to achieve more while I was in high school. I started to do my homework and really felt like Lincoln was the school to be at if I wanted to attend a Division I college to play football and obtain a degree. Although NFC has a strong reputation for doing the same thing, Lincoln had a bigger platform for me.

I went home to speak with my parents after my sophomore season, and my dad supported my decision to attend Lincoln to gain more exposure for my football career. Lincoln also had a strong advanced placement program to take college courses that would prepare me for the next stages of my life just in case football did not work out. I had all these points solidified in addition to rankings or statistics for my mom to view, but she was not buying anything my father and I had to say about Lincoln.

Finally, my mother agreed, and I was able to withdraw from NFC at the end of my sophomore year to attend Lincoln. This was one of the toughest decisions I had to make in my young career because I literally grew up with my teammates at NFC since I was four years old. Something felt weird leaving them behind, but I wanted to really see how good I was as a football player.

After I arrived at Lincoln, I began to see it was not going to be a smooth transition for me. At NFC, I was one of the big men on campus because I was one of the fastest and most skilled guys on the team. Then I went to my first workout at Lincoln, and I could not believe what I was seeing. I said to myself, there is no way I am going to be able to make it here. I even contemplated going back to NFC over the summer to get my spot back and most likely win a state title.

I decided to stay at Lincoln and make the adjustment to become a key contributor for the Trojans. The road was not easy, and I had to wait for my turn. But when I got my opportunity, I seized the moment, and I never looked back.

It seems like yesterday when I was gearing up for one of the biggest moments of my life. As a young boy, I grew up idolizing collegiate football and dreaming of playing collegiate football at the highest level. Every Saturday, I started my day off by watching ESPN's College Game Day and wondering what helmet Lee Corso would place on his head for that particular week. From that moment on, I knew I wanted to play collegiate football and experience the excitement I saw on the show. It taught me that collegiate football was not just a hobby; for some people, it was a lifestyle.

I really began to prepare myself mentally and physically to obtain this goal of playing collegiate football. At the conclusion of my junior year, I began to receive letters from different colleges daily. That is when I knew my dream was on the verge of happening.

I can vividly remember when I received my first collegiate letter from the Division III powerhouse Mount Union Purple Raiders. I was so elated that I called my dad at his job to let him know that I was on someone's radar for my athletic ability. This day was a milestone in my life. Most of my teammates were receiving letters from powerhouse schools such as Florida State, Florida, Alabama, Georgia, Southern California, Texas, and other notable programs. But I knew if I continued to work hard, I would receive that same attention from the schools that carry a lot of equity.

As I predicted, the letters began to roll in weekly, and it was a different school each week. Some sent handwritten notes from notable coaches, referencing how much of an impact I could make for their university. This experience was truly a humbling one, and I was grateful for this opportunity as I went through the recruiting process.

Many of you can resonate with me about how fast the mail begins to pile up. One thing I always had to do to remain grounded was remind myself that there is always someone better than me in everything. Remain humble and hungry and always work hard because you never know when a season or career-ending injury can occur. When the letters come in, it makes you work harder at practice, and it shows that your hard work is paying off. I would stay after practice and do additional sprints to make sure I was in shape to endure the fourth quarter, or I would do extra footwork drills to help improve my skills. No matter what it was, I wanted to out work everyone and my mentality was to be the best.

Being recruited by some of the most notable programs in collegiate football was something that was truly special to me. Having the opportunity to meet and interact with different coaches was simply something that I would never trade in the world. I was fortunate to have over twenty-five offers to attend Division I schools to play collegiate football and obtain my degree. I knew that football was not going to sustain me for the rest of my life, so I ended up taking official visits to University of California- Los Angeles,

University of Mississippi, and Michigan State University for academic and personal reasons as well.

I narrowed it down to these three schools by the criteria of graduation rates, playing time, family atmosphere, and many other minor details that would help me make my decision. This process can also be very stressful, and the fun gets taken out of it because the media is so heavily involved with your decision. Many coaches call you to boost your ego, and all the letters and other communications can be a bit overwhelming at times. This is especially true when you are trying to focus on finishing high school with a strong GPA and enjoying those once in a lifetime moments. I decided that I was going to make a decision before signing day to help alleviate some of the pressure of where I was going to spend the next four years of my life. Finally I was one week away, and the time had come to solidify my decision.

I began to reflect upon all the hard work, time, and discipline it took to achieve my goal of signing a national letter of intent. On February 2, 2006, I was finally about to make my own dream a reality. It was time for me to claim my reward and everything that I worked so hard for since I was four years old. It was my time to stand up and make the announcement on where I was going to play Division I football. To be honest, I knew where to go; everything felt just right.

This was a very special moment for me. I remember vividly how everything happened that day. I stood up and thanked God first for blessing me with the talent to play this game, and then I thanked my parents and my beautiful girlfriend who is now my wife and everyone who helped me achieve my goal of signing this letter of intent. The wait was finally over and I said, "The school that I chose to attend is…Michigan State University!" As I was finishing my statement, the MSU fight song began to play at my high school assembly, and my peers and family members were ecstatic. Immediately, I felt goose bumps pop up on every inch of my body, and I was ready to run through a wall for MSU.

I was officially a Michigan State Spartan and was immediately embraced by fans via Spartan Mag, Spartan Tailgate, Go Green Go White Blog, and many other publications that embodied Michigan State athletics. It was very hard to fathom that I was on the front page of the website of the Lansing State Journal! It was truly an honor, and I could not believe that my dream was a reality. I had finally obtained my goal, and this was indeed one of the happiest moments of my life. After the announcement, I went out to eat and celebrate with my friends and family who came to my high school's signing day assembly. The next day, I went right back to training and preparing myself to officially get ready to join the Spartan Nation.

A few days later, I received my workout manual. I was eager to open it and start my new workout regimen. I knew I was going to need some additional help to understand these different defensive schemes and it seemed as though the book was written in another language when I tried to review it myself. I was very fortunate to have my high school defensive back coach help me understand the plays and get acclimated to becoming a collegiate football player. Even though he played for another Big Ten foe, the Minnesota Golden Gophers, he was more than willing to help a future Spartan capture success.

I truly believe that life is about relationships, and there is nothing like a player-coach relationship. Words cannot express how much I appreciate Coach Saunders and all he did to prepare me for collegiate football. We all have someone in our lives who has pushed us because they saw something inside of us that we did not see in ourselves. I had my work cut out for me because I was only 177 lbs, and I needed to bulk up to 190 lbs before I headed north for Big Ten country. If not, I was going to get bounced around like a pinball on Saturdays. I had four months to achieve my goal and make sure I was in the best shape of my life before I headed to East Lansing.

I literally did everything my workout manual told me to do daily, and I was determined to make an immediate impact as a freshman. Coach Saunders would share stories with me about how college will be completely different from high school, and there is not much margin for error or else you will be replaced. He also was very frank about coaches and their recruiting spiels and how they all say whatever it takes to get you there. You should realize that once you have signed, things may change because you have already fulfilled your commitment to them.

Make sure you are going to the school because you want to be there, not for a specific coach. Collegiate football is a business, and your coach could be gone as soon as you arrive because that is how the industry works. So ask yourself this question: would I attend this school regardless of which coach is here? You have to make sure you pick an institution that you are comfortable with and somewhere you can excel in all facets of your career. That was my mindset when I chose Michigan State University.

Travis

Growing up as a young kid in Harvey, IL in the early 90s, basketball was king. Michael Jordan and the Bulls were on top of the world, and every young kid within a hundred-mile radius of the United Center had a basketball in hand, singing the famous tune of "Like Mike, if I could be like Mike!" To be honest, the only reason I considered playing football was to stay active and out of trouble when basketball season was over. I have always been a fan of the game itself, but it never really made a difference to me if I played or not.

All that began to change one July afternoon in 1995 when my Uncle Bill piled me into his old Chevrolet Blazer along with my brother William and my cousin William and drove us down to Ashland Park to sign up to play Pop Warner football for the Harvey Colts. The Colts are a storied program that at the time had already produced Division I and NFL players such as Tia Streets, Sammie Williams, Barry Gardner, Napoleon Harris, and Antwaan Randle El. Little did I know, my name would later be added to this list of great players.

After a few more rough years in Harvey, my mom decided that it was in the best interest of my brother and me to move away from its chaotic streets to Three Rivers, MI as we headed into high school. This experience was the definition of a complete culture shock. I went from attending a school with a population of 99 percent blacks to a school where I was the only kid of any minority race in my second-hour science class. I went from kicking empty beer cans for four blocks on my walk to school to kicking stones down a quarter mile dirt road just to make it to the bus stop, where an hour long bus ride awaited me! Needless to say, I didn't know if I was going to last long. It was not where I wanted to be, but I knew that with hard work and focus, it would give me the fresh start that my mom was so desperately seeking for me!

As the school year began, my mom told me that I was only allowed to play one sport, and that she wanted me to focus on getting my grades up. Of course the sport that I chose was my first love – basketball! In reality, I was a pretty good basketball player who was in denial about the fact that football was clearly my best sport. I just went with where my heart was at that time! I would miss the next two football seasons leading into my freshman year of high school before my mom decided to let me play football and basketball again in the same year.

I quickly realized that the beauty of living in a small town in southwest Michigan is that everyone was overly passionate about high school football, and if you were good at it, you were king. Three Rivers football was a big deal in our area, and we had a reputation for having great athletes and winning. I was proud to be a part of this culture and finally began to settle into this new environment.

I began to surround myself with people who had the same interest and focus as I did — sports, making honest money, and keeping good grades. I would often hang out with my brother William and his friends Calvin, Duane, Marshall, and Ronnie Jr. who were all older than me. We all had a lot in common from our family backgrounds and religious views to what toppings we liked on our pizzas.

Naturally, I found myself hanging out with Calvin more and more even when my brother wasn't around. We even started our own landscaping business together, hauling my old riding mower around town on a trailer that was hitched to the back of his old 1986 Oldsmobile Delta station wagon. This business venture built trust between us, and for the next three years in high school, we were pretty much inseparable.

Duane and I were pretty close as well. Our mothers became best friends, and that drew us closer together. We were like family. Athletically, Duane was the most gifted athlete in Three Rivers, and to this day, one of the most gifted athletes I have ever been around.

Ronnie was an extremely hard worker and very athletic as well. Outside of sports, we spent most of our time together cleaning floors for his family's commercial cleaning business. Marshall was not much of an athlete but was a very gifted musician. He was the best keyboard player I had ever met and at that time had not learned to read a music note. He truly had a gift from God. All of these guys where talented in one area or another and were determined to make something of their lives just like I was.

I am a firm believer in the ole saying "You are who you surround yourself with!" These guys were the most competitive people I knew, outside of myself of course. We challenged each other at everything; it didn't matter what it was. We took tremendous pride in trying to outwork each other on every level. From NFL 2K on the Dreamcast to skipping rocks across the Saint Joseph River. Everything was a battle. We put boxing gloves on every weekend and beat each other's brains in trying to prove who had the best hands. The gridiron, the hardwood, and the track was where most of our competitions took place. We turned each other into great athletes and winners by having individual battles. We built a bond that still holds strong to this day.

This competitive environment we created poured into our academics as well. I can remember studying for hours upon hours with Calvin for exams. I would leave his house, go home, and study for the rest of the night just to make sure I got one percent higher than he did on the exam. The next day, we would both ask if the other did any extra studying and we would both lie through our teeth, and say no! We both knew how competitive the other person was and did everything in our power to gain an edge.

Unfortunately, where we played ball wasn't a hot bed for recruiting. You rarely see a player go to or even be recruited by a Division I school, but these guys had talent. I can remember my sophomore year when Calvin and Duane both began to receive recruiting letters in the mail from different colleges and universities. It was a very exciting time for both of them. Most of Calvin's interest came from Division II and III schools. In my mind, he definitely had the ability and the brains to play at the Division I level. With academics being his main focus, Calvin decided that he was going to attend Alma College, one of the best Liberal Arts colleges in the country, and play football.

Duane on the other hand received a lot Division I interest from multiple schools. Watching him be recruited was the first exposure I had to the process. I even had the chance to go on a couple of official visits with him, which was cool. Duane ended up accepting a full ride to Central Michigan University.

By my junior year, I had not received any interest to play football at the next level. However, due to the strong influence of my girlfriend, Giovanna (now my wife), family, my group of friends, and a few teachers, going to college was definitely a reality for me, and Michigan State University was the only place I wanted to attend! At that moment, an athletic scholarship was not looking like my ticket in. I was very confident in my football ability, but not being recruited after a very productive junior season told me that my academics would have to get me to the door.

I began to focus solely on what I need to do from an academic standpoint to get into Michigan State. I figured if the Michigan State football coaches wouldn't come to me, I would go to them. If I could just make my way on campus, I would be able to prove that I was good enough to play football at that level.

I restructured my class schedule and got more involved in community service activities. I even got involved with a few student body programs to build my resume. Studying for the ACT exam became a normal part of my everyday routine. I ended up taking the exam twice my junior year before I secured a score that was good enough to meet Michigan State's standards.

Putting extra energy and effort into my academics didn't detour me from the work I knew I had to put in to make sure I was physically ready *when my opportunity presented itself. Ronnie's dad, Big Ron, played a vital role in this preparation. Big Ron was known around town as being a weight room guru. As I mentioned before, he gave me the opportunity to work for his commercial cleaning business to earn some extra cash.*

Big Ron and I spent a lot of nights together, working and talking about life. It was through these conversations that Big Ron saw how determined I was to achieve my goal of attending and playing for Michigan State. He assured me every single day that I could do it and promised to do everything in his power to make sure I was physically and mentally prepared. Big Ron and I spent time in the weight room every day before work, lifting and running. I thought I knew what it meant to "grind," but Big Ron opened my eyes to a whole new reality!

Heading into the fall of my senior year, I still had not received any interest to play football in college. However, I did get the one confirmation that I had been truly seeking. It was official, I was accepted into the College of Engineering at Michigan State University! It is still up to this day one of my most proud moments in life! I knew at that moment, I was in the driver's seat for creating a future for myself, and the sky was the limit to what I could become.

My final football season at Three Rivers High was amazing. I lead my team to a two loss record and a deep run in the state playoffs, earning numerous accolades along the way. After the season was over, I began to receive interest from a few small colleges that wanted me to come and play football. Taking visits to those schools confirmed that Michigan State was the only place for me.

I made up my mind that if I couldn't play football at the highest level, I didn't want to play at all! It was as simple as that. Football is a part of who I am. Living without football at that time was not an option; therefore, not making the team at Michigan State was not an option! I approached everyday with that mindset. With Big Ron pushing me, I continued to work my tail off, preparing for my big day.

I can remember vividly the night I moved into my dorm room in Brody Complex. It was a very emotional moment for my family and Gia. With all of that going on, the only thing I could find myself thinking about was finding out where I needed to go the next morning to talk to the head coach, John L. Smith.

My family took off to head back home, and later that night, I walked over to the Duffy Daugherty Football Building to look around and get my game plan together. I had everything mapped out to the tee. I played the meeting with the Coach Smith out in my head a million times and knew exactly what I wanted to say to him. It was all going to work out. The feeling was right!

The next morning, I woke up bright and early! I headed over to the Duff and marched confidently in the front door. I was greeted at the front desk by the receptionist, Cindy, who asked if I needed help finding my way. I anxiously told her that I wanted to speak to the Coach Smith about walking on to the team and asked if she could show me where I could find him.

Little did I know, the news that I was about to receive was not going to play out the way that I had pictured it the night before. I was not going to walk into the head coach's office, tell him my story, and walk out with a date and time to show up for the next practice. What Cindy told me was definitely not what I wanted to hear, but the way she handled the situation led to the beginning of a very special relationship between the two of us that still exists.

Recognizing how much courage it just took for me to walk through those double doors, Cindy proceeded to tell me that I had already missed the open tryouts for the fall. She expressed how sorry she was and informed me that there would be another tryout at the beginning of spring semester. She wrote my contact information down on a sticky note and promised me that she would let me know exactly when the tryout would be. I thanked her and disappointedly walked away. I couldn't believe it! After all the hard work I put in waiting for that day to come, I walked away only with a promise to be called back from the secretary. It was not a good start to my so called new beginning!

That night, I called Calvin to tell him how everything thing went. After giving him the details of my chat with Cindy, he quickly responded with, "Hey, at least you still have a chance. Make sure you are ready when she calls you back!" At that moment, I was quickly over feeling sorry for myself and got back to the drawing board. I thought about all the grinding and sacrifices I had made up to that point and reminded myself that failure was not an option for me!

The next morning, I got up and went over to the intramural building and paid for a gym pass. Big Ron had already given me all the knowledge I needed to stay on top of my game. It was all up to me at this point to prove to myself how bad I wanted to achieve my goal. For the next semester, I would spend almost every night at the IM, lifting weights and running.

People would often ask me why I was training so hard or what I was training for. I would always respond to them saying, "So that you can watch me run out of the tunnel in the Spartan Stadium next fall." Most of the time, I got the "oh ok" or the "ha, good luck with that" response. Not many people believed me when I told them what I was going to do.

Those doubters just gave me a little more motivation to keep pushing. That fall, I turned down many opportunities to go to home football games at Spartan Stadium. I promised myself that the next time I walked into that stadium I would be a member of the team. You better believe that a free ticket to watch the battle for the Paul Bunyan Trophy against the University of Michigan wasn't going to make me break that promise!

My first semester of college flew by. Every day was a new experience. The social scene in East Lansing is second to none, and I had the opportunity to meet and get to know new people from all over the world. I was having the time of my life. To top it off, I was able to prove to myself that I could be competitive academically at this level. I finished the fall semester with a 3.8 GPA. I had a lot going on, but I never lost sight of my goal to play for the Green and White. I counted down every second until the end of the semester when I would find out if Cindy was going to keep her promise.

Winter break quickly came and went. I was happy to have a break from school, but I couldn't wait to get it over with so that I could finally get what I had been working for. The night I got back to campus, I checked my e-mail, hoping to see my inbox flashing with a message from Cindy. There was nothing. For a split second, I thought, What if she just balled up my information and threw it in the trash? After all, she must get hundreds of hopefuls coming through those doors every day, right? Was it just her routine to be nice and send us on our way?

In that moment, I thought there was no way this lady is going to go out of her way to contact me. I quickly stopped pondering over that idea and called it a night. I woke up early the next day and went straight to the computer. I checked my e-mail and at last had a message in my inbox from Cindy. She wrote, "I hope you didn't think I forgot about you" and proceeded to give me the details of when and where the tryout was going to be held. I couldn't believe it! This woman kept her word to me, someone she had never met before, after all this time!

I continued to get myself ready over the next couple of days, running routes and doing defensive back drills. I even had a kid from my dorm floor punting to me so that I would be ready for that in case it was a part of the workout. My time was coming, and I wanted to make sure that I was sharp on every level! I didn't want anyone to show me up during this tryout. I knew in my heart that no one had prepared like I had for this opportunity, and I was ready to prove that I was worthy of a chance.

When I walked into the indoor practice facility for the first time, chills ran through my body. I said a few prayers and took a few moments alone to reflect on all I had done to prepare for that very moment. There was no doubt in my mind I was ready.

About fifty to sixty students came, in the hopes of becoming a Division I athlete. I knew that it would be a big turn out because I read an article in the student newspaper, the State News, a couple of days earlier, inviting people to come out. I recognized a few guys that I worked out with at the IM and noticed a few others who I can guarantee you hadn't run since high school. None of them mattered to me at that time. I was completely focused on showing that I had enough talent to play here!

Coach Ken Mannie, the Head Strength Coach, pulled us all together, explained how the day was going to go, and took us through the workout. I made sure that I was the first guy in line for every single drill we went through that day. I ended up doing twice as many reps as everyone else because Coach Mannie wanted me to demonstrate every drill before taking my normal reps. I was completely fine with it knowing that I was getting an opportunity to show what kind of leader I was.

Coach Mannie tried to destroy us that day. Not many people made it through the day without dropping out of a drill or bending over and exposing how tired they were. I had way too much pride to let myself go out like that! At the end of the workout, Coach Mannie told us that someone from his staff would contact us if we passed through that phase of making the team. He proceeded to tell us how there weren't many spots open, and it was highly possible that none of us would make the cut. Although confident and proud of the effort I just displayed, I left that workout nervous and unsure if I would get a call.

A few days went by with no word. The anticipation of just finding out my fate, either way, was driving me crazy. And then my phone rang! It was Coach Mannie calling to tell me that I made the cut. It turned out I was the only one who tried out that made it! He went on to make it very clear this was only the first step, and I still had a long road ahead of me before I was actually on the team. He explained that I had to prove myself worthy to the coaches during winter conditioning in order to get invited back for spring ball. After passing that phase, I would have to perform well enough in spring ball to *get an invite back to fall camp. The last step would be to outperform some of the scholarship players in fall camp to become a member of the 2004 Michigan State Spartans!*

As he was explaining this long road ahead, none of it intimidated me at all. I knew that I could play the game! I knew that I was a great student and a great person! I knew that I had already put in the work and prepared for this opportunity! And most importantly, I knew that I wasn't going to let anyone in that locker room work harder than me, ever! In my mind, failure was never an option! At that very moment, I knew that I was going to be a Division I football player for the Michigan State University Spartans!

FAST PACE

In college athletics, time for rest or relaxation is minimal in or out of season. Many student-athletes are blinded by the fact that playing collegiate football is a full-time commitment, basically a job. There are four segments of training that you will be involved in throughout the year. They consist of winter conditioning, spring ball, summer conditioning, and weight training throughout the year.

As soon as you arrive on campus, you will hit the ground running by training with the team. This will be your first true test to see exactly where you stand amongst the rest of the guys. You will be thrown into the fire to see if you have been utilizing your workout manual. Trust us when we say that if you have not been working out, you will be exposed in front of your new teammates. You don't want to start your career on a bad note. This is your opportunity to set the tone for your career as a collegiate athlete!

∞

Ashton

I can remember vividly running sprints on Ralph Young Field and almost passing out. The sad thing about it was we were just finishing the warm up and calisthenics portion of the workout. Everything was moving at a rapid pace, and I was feeling a bit overwhelmed as you will feel during your first workout.

Travis

You have to be mentally tough at this point. I would often go through workouts, repeating to myself over and over again "Mind over matter!" You have to control your body with your mind, not the other way around! The only way you can assure that your mind won't fail you in the heat of the battle is to prepare ahead of time.

It takes time to get acclimated to a different workout style and new coaches who believe there is no such thing as half speed. Everything in college is always done full speed and with meticulous attention to detail. It sounds a little cliché, but the little things end up getting you beat. You are put in tough situations every day to see how you will respond in the fourth quarter. When your team goes to overtime or experiences some adversity during the game, how will you respond? All of the skill sets you are learning during these phases are transferable onto the field.

There will be plenty of situations in the game where you have to dig deep to make that stop on 4th and 1, or just make a play when your team needs it the most. Whenever you find yourself staring adversity in the face, always reflect back on prior battles. One of two things had to have happened; you either stepped up to the plate, or you gave in. The times you defeated the challenge proves that you are capable. If you ever gave up or threw in the towel, I am sure those moments are still haunting you to this day! Both situations can be effective motivators on moving forward.

One thing you cannot do is try to get through these workouts alone. You may also have to lean on upperclassmen for guidance because they have been in your shoes before. It's tough to come into a new environment and jump right into doing things at such a rapid pace. Chances are the older guys know what to expect. Rely on your teammates to help pull you through these tough times. Fighting through pain together helps take your focus away from the agony your body will be experiencing.

Travis

Nothing got me more energized than encouraging a struggling teammate to keep fighting and pressing on! When I would see that my teammates needed a boost of energy during a workout, I would yell at the top of my voice, "Time to crank up...crrrraaaaaaaaaaank!" My teammates would respond by yelling, "crrrraaaaaaaaaaank!" It might sound crazy but doing this gave us all a little jolt of energy every time. It also built camaraderie between us and reassured us that we were all in it together.

∞

During these times, it helps that you build relationships with your teammates and really mold chemistry amongst the team. It does not matter how much individual talent is on your team at all. If you do not have chemistry, your team will not be successful. This is when your teammates find out if they can trust you, and you find out if they are trustworthy!

Ashton

I have been on teams that had great talent but just could not gel together at all. Everyone seemed to focus on padding their stats instead of focusing on the best interest of the team. Contrary to that, I have been on teams where many would say we lacked talent and depth but experienced success because of our chemistry.

The situation compares to what takes place in the atomic structure. The team is your nucleus, and the players and coaches are the protons and neutrons, working together to provide the positive energy and direction of the atom, celebrating everyone's achievements along the way. You can achieve so many great things in football and in life if you learn to put your pride aside and invest in others around you.

It is important you understand that there are many highly talented individuals playing collegiate football. Not all of their success is due to their natural ability, but in part, a reflection of great attention to detail in other areas of preparation, such as film study, mastering proper technique, and simply being coachable at all times.

Breaking down film is not as simple as it sounds. You must spend just as much time looking at the film of yourself and teammates as you do scouting an opponent. It involves discipline and a true understanding of the game. If you don't know and understand what you are looking for, you will not be able to critique and correct what you are looking at. It is crucial that you understand your playbook and what your coaches are looking for in your technique before you go into a film session alone. If you don't, you won't be productive during the session.

Mastering the technique that is being coached is another key to elevating your game. This comes not only in film and teaching sessions with your coaches but with spending time on your own getting repetitions. You must put in extra time sharpening your tools in order to separate your ability from the rest of the packs. At this level, you will not have time to think about how you should be moving, it has to become second nature. If you can't master that, you will be beat at the snap of the ball! Getting your body to react and respond with the right technique in the heat of the game takes time and reps.

It has always been known that when a coach is riding your butt hard, he sees your potential to be great. You must have thick skin and not take hard nose coaching personal. Constructive criticism is a difficult thing to understand as a young player. Being composed and maintaining positive body language relays to the coach that you are coachable and serious about getting better. The faster you learn how to deal with this concept, the better off you will be. You should be worried when a coach is not paying you any attention! As you embark upon this fast-paced journey, it is important that you often reflect on the hard work it took to get to this point. You must be prepared to work ten times harder to achieve greatness at this next level.

ACCOUNTABILITY

Being a college athlete comes with a lot of responsibility. This responsibility includes holding yourself to a high standard and being accountable to your family, your school, and your team. There will be extremely high standards set for you that you must live up too. From the way that you practice and play the game to the way that you conduct yourself in non-football environments, high expectations will be in place for you to meet. You will be expected day in and day out to put forth the effort that is necessary to be the best person, the best student, and the best athlete that you can be.

There are people in your personal life who played a huge part in making sure that you were prepared for this opportunity because they love you. Your coaches will have to pass up on hundreds of other athletes to give you a chance because they believe in you. Your teammates are the ones who will make sacrifices and go through the blood, sweat, and tears with you so that you all can achieve success on and off the field. These people will hold you accountable for every move and decision that you make because they all have invested in you to some degree. What you do from this point on and who you become will not only affect you but will impact all the people mentioned above as well.

Travis

This reminds me of a quote that echoed in the locker room of the Indianapolis Colts when I played there in 2009. Super Bowl winning and soon-to-be Hall of Fame Coach Tony Dungy, who was already retired at that time, would always say, "No excuses. No explanations! Just do your job!" This mindset held everyone in the organization accountable for what their responsibility was. It didn't matter if you were the equipment manager, the front desk receptionist, or Peyton Manning, if you executed your job with meticulous focus and effort, the organization would be successful. At the end of the day, no one expected to hear any excuses or explanations for why your work turned out the way it did, good or bad. Everyone expected you to take ownership of your piece to the puzzle and the outcome of your performance.

DISCIPLINE & DECISION MAKING

There will be many times throughout your collegiate career when you are going to have to make some tough choices—choices that will make or break your career. There are plenty of talented athletes across the country who are plagued with poor decision-making. Decisions such as participating in bar fights, domestic disputes, drinking and driving, underage drinking, and utilizing street drugs that have completely detoured them from the path of success. These guys lack discipline and usually don't last long!

It is vital for you to understand that the decisions you make affect more people than just you. When you get in trouble, your respective university is tarnished, your home town is embarrassed, and most importantly, your family name is shamed. You represent everyone who has ever loved you, helped you, believed in you, or went out of their way to make sure you made something of yourself. To these people, you hold a responsibility to make the right decision every single time!

Most bad decisions are made due to impulsive behavior. This means that bad decisions are the result of acting before thinking. Warren Buffet, one of the world's most successful businessmen, sums it up, saying, "It takes twenty years to build a reputation and five minutes to ruin it!" No matter how heated the moment is, you must always reserve the discipline to stop and think before you react. Stop and ask yourself: would this decision make my parents proud? Will this make my teammates and coaches proud? Will this make my university proud? If the answer is anything close to no, you need to walk away. This is a very important element you have to understand before you come to college.

Ashton

My parents instilled in me to always be my own man and make the right choices. There were times when I had to stand alone because I knew it was the right thing to do. I was definitely far from being a perfect person, but one thing that I can honestly say is I processed everything before I did it. I made sure that the decision I made would not be detrimental to my family, my school, or my team.

Travis

I was taught at a young age that a good name is priceless. The reason that my name is good is not because of me but because of all the people before me who dignified it. I have a responsibility to those who have paved the way for me to be in the position I am in today and not to disgrace our family's name.

So many talented guys bring their past with them when they come to college. They feel obligated to act out or prove they are a tough guy because of where they are from. This can be detrimental to the relationships you have with teammates, coaches, and others around your school. You must embrace the opportunity to be in a new place with new faces and new standards. Become who you want to be, and don't let your past set limitations. Leave all the drama back at home and make the best of everything you are blessed with.

The best way to ensure you make good decisions is to surround yourself with honest and positive people. When you have friends who value doing the right thing, a positive environment is created, and your collegiate football experience will be positive. They will help keep you grounded by always telling you the truth even when you do not want to hear it. It's hard to find people who will keep it real with you like this. If you can't find them, just make sure you carry yourself this way. You will be surprised how many people will follow suit.

It's essential to gravitate toward positive people who share the same goals and ideals you possess. These teammates will remain in your circle and have your back, even when your playing days are over.

A very common scenario in collegiate football is going out and partying after the big win on a Saturday night. This is something that most football players around the country struggle with on a weekly basis. There is nothing wrong with celebrating with your teammates after a big win. However, you have to make smart decisions when you do.

Ashton

In 2008, we won a big game against the University of Wisconsin with a last minute field goal. Brett Swenson was one the best kickers I have ever played with. It was nothing but pandemonium when he nailed the kick from forty-four yards out. After the excitement died down, I had a bigger decision to tackle that night.

I had a big exam on Monday that I needed to do well on. I will let you guys guess what decision I made! Yeah...I went out with my teammates to celebrate our win. I concluded in my head that I was fine because I was pretty familiar with the material. It turned out to be not a smart choice on my part. I ended up doing horrible on my exam and was truly disappointed in myself for not having discipline at the time. It was truly a good learning experience for me because I made sure that I did not make the same mistake again. There will be plenty of parties to attend *in college, so do not put yourself in situations like this one.*

      There are tons of different scenarios you will encounter as a college student-athlete. You may not experience these exact situations, but no matter what you face, tough decisions will have to be made at some point. Please take time and start understanding the type of person and player you want to become. Applying these concepts to prepare you for making good decisions can keep you on the right path. Decision making is very important in all that you do because you control your own destiny. Always remember that it's easy to get in trouble, but hard to get out of it.

TIME MANAGEMENT

An essential piece to ensuring a successful transition to the next level is your time management skills. There are many players who are good with managing their time and many who are horrible. If you have a problem with keeping yourself on task, you are going to be in for a rude awakening when you come to play collegiate football. Every day is a race against time.

As soon as you report to your university, you will be handed a block schedule that will have your day planned from 5:45 AM–9:30 PM. This schedule will detail all that you are required to attend each day with locations and times. Everything from breakfast, early morning workouts, classes and tutors, to study table at night will be included. As a freshman, this structure is definitely something that can get overwhelming very quickly, and you may experience the feeling of wanting to quit.

Your every step is mapped out. You have to prove that you are responsible enough to handle these obligations. Your parents or legal guardians will not be there anymore to wake you up and help you out. You are expected to do whatever it takes to be present and on time for everything on your schedule. Expect to be held accountable if you are late to anything for any reason.

Travis

The Coach Mannie would always say to us, "If you are not ten minutes early you are late!" This was the expectation set for our program and everyone, including coaches and trainers, were held accountable.

This is a part of becoming an adult and standing on your own two feet. Structure is a good habit to embrace and will be beneficial in your personal life as well. You guys are probably wondering when you will find time for a social life. The reality is there will be very limited time for you to enjoy yourself socially. Your schedule is just too demanding. You are in school to obtain your degree as well as play football at a high level. That must remain your focus. Your collegiate football experience will be one of the most exciting times in your life and well worth missing a few parties.

When you sign that letter of intent or walk-on to a football program, you automatically inherit a great deal of responsibility and expectation. It's definitely a commitment to sacrifice some aspects of your collegiate experience for something greater than yourself. This ability to make such a sacrifice is a huge contributor to what people like to call the It Factor, which separates the college student-athlete and everyone else. Most students on campus could not handle the rigorous lifestyle of a collegiate football player. Just being athletic isn't enough. You must possess other intangibles as well in order to do this each and every day.

There is a campus event at MSU called Bridging the Gap between Athletes and Students that we commend for helping the entire student body understand the life of a student-athlete. This program is geared to change the way non-student-athletes view student-athletes and help them understand how hard we actually work and manage our time. There is a panel of student-athletes who address the students about our rigorous schedule and the day-to-day operations. Many students are completely shocked that we are up at 5 AM for training. It really helps when everyone understands that nothing is just given to us.

Hard work does pay off, and you must trust there will be plenty of opportunities to meet ladies and simply enjoy the college experience. You have to make sure your priorities are in order, and things will fall into place. The schedule blocks will decrease each year if you show maturity and prove that you can handle yourself without supervision. Some guys choose to have their own agendas and end up causing headaches for the coaching and academic support staff. This will lead to your collegiate experience being very unpleasant.

It is recommended to start setting aside time to get yourself acclimated to the new structure you will encounter before you show up on campus. Try to map out all the obligations and commitments you have throughout the week. Set a schedule with dates, times, and locations of where it is you need to be. Challenge yourself by including a few things that are not current obligations such as extra running or studying. The key here is to schedule all events before your week begins and stick to the schedule. If you don't, things will come up, and you will begin to procrastinate. Remember, when you get to college, you won't be able to shuffle things around. The schedule is set, and no matter what comes up, you are expected to follow it to a tee. Doing this will not be as extensive but will help to prepare you for what lies ahead in college.

Managing your time is very essential for your growth and development at the next level. You have to utilize your resources and make sure you stay on task in order to be successful. It's imperative to show that you are responsible, and that you can handle yourself without supervision. Once you get a semester under your belt, things will feel a lot better, and you will not feel as overwhelmed. Before you know it, it will be your turn to lend advice to the incoming freshmen on how to overcome this challenging time in your life.

FINDING A BALANCE

There is an old saying that has resonated for quite some time now, "Different strokes for different folks." This is basically saying that there is more than one formula for success. Everyone's path may be a little different, and each step even more unique, but we can all experience the same success at the end of the day. You just have to figure out what works best for you in terms of how you balance school, football, and your personal life.

You will need to develop your own habits. It is perfectly fine to look to the upperclassmen for guidance, but what they do might not work for you. Just because your roommate is successful studying for exams at night doesn't mean that same strategy will work for you. You may find that you retain information better when you wake up early in the morning to look over the material. Being in a quiet room at the library may help you focus better as opposed to studying in your dorm room. Watching film right after practice may benefit you more than watching it later in the evening. You might go through dozens of trial and error periods before you figure out what works best for you.

Ashton

I learned many valuable lessons in college, but one of the most beneficial lessons was being able to find a balance for myself. I made countless mistakes trying to emulate what many of my teammates did because a lot of their strategies did not lead to success for me. Being on a football team gives you the chance to broaden your horizons and assimilate to various cultures. There is always room to learn new things and see how upperclassmen handle their own schedules. I can remember trying to add things to my regimen that just did not work for me at all. These things included studying with music, staying up late, and other activities that worked for my teammates. It's imperative that you find what works for your own level of comfort.

I had to find my own niche to make my experience more enjoyable. I am the type of person who must have structure at all times. Many of my close friends can attest to this and will be glad to tell *you how particular I am about having things in order. As a freshman, I learned a method from my academic mentor at MSU, Danielle Lesure, which helped to keep my academics in order. She showed me how to create structure for myself and produce free time by taking care of business ahead of time. She taught me the importance of utilizing a monthly calendar to stay on top of my tasks and responsibilities. This gives me something tangible for reference when planning out how each day is going to go. I still utilize this strategy in my personal and professional life today.*

These same concepts apply when dealing with your personal and social life. You cannot let anyone else dictate how you spend your time. Peer pressure is hard to overcome at your age, and you will be challenged daily. Be your own person, and know your limits. Do I go out to the club tonight, or do I stay in and study for my upcoming exam? Do I stay up all night playing video games with teammates, or do I hit the sack and make sure to get the proper amount of rest? Do I stay and watch extra film, or do I head straight to my girlfriend's place after practice? These are the decisions that you will face. It is important that you are ready to face options similar to the ones mentioned above at some point. You must figure out what, when, and how all these things will fit in your schedule in a way that you don't fall off track. How you position these things into your schedule will make all the difference.

Every so often you will come across a teammate who seems to be able to pull off having a crazy, unorganized social life and still manages to perform well on the field. These cases are very rare, and you should avoid trying to emulate their habits. You can rest assured that another area of their life, most likely their academics, is suffering behind the scenes.

Travis

I had a teammate who could not keep a healthy balance between enjoying the social scene in East Lansing and keeping up with his school work and football responsibilities. This guy would spend four to five of the seven nights in a week hanging out in the local bars. He was what most would consider a "party animal." Somehow, he always managed to make it to practice and workout sessions and perform pretty well day in and day out. The majority of the time he was hung over or still drunk and never seemed to skip a beat. He seemed to have everything under control. Intellectually, he was a pretty bright guy; so when he started to miss time because of academic reasons, it was clear that it wasn't because he wasn't smart enough for college level courses. This guy just didn't have his priorities in line. He spent so much time hanging out that he never gave himself time to study and do homework. The next season, it all caught up to him, and he ended up getting kicked off the team because of poor academic performance.

Time is an extremely valuable element. It is inevitable that you will struggle with managing it at some point while you are in college. Although football takes up a significant amount of your time, you will have some time to yourself. What you decide to do with your time can make or break your collegiate experience. You have to set yourself up on a successful road early in your career.

Many people use the term student-athlete loosely, but you really have to be a student first and an athlete second if you plan to succeed. Proving to your coaches and support staff that you are mature enough to make smart decisions as a freshman will allow you to have more free time down the road. However, if you are a knucklehead, you will always have someone looking over your shoulder because you cannot be trusted. Taking advantage of the opportunity to prove you can balance your own schedule early in your career will lead to a more enjoyable experience.

CREATING A POSITIVE ENVIRONMENT

As mentioned in the previous chapters, coming in as a freshman your life will be mapped out and planned for you. However, it is important to understand that you are the ultimate decision maker of how you spend your time. People are getting paid to make sure that you are guided down the right path, but you have the freedom to decide whether or not to buy in and take the actual steps in that direction. If you choose to go against the grain, it is almost a guarantee that you won't last long on your team, and that you will create other problems and situations for yourself that won't be easy to overcome.

In order to ensure a successful collegiate experience, it is important that you create a positive environment around yourself that will lead to you making good, healthy decisions personally, academically, and athletically. You need to seek out people who have positive attitudes and share some of the same goals and aspirations as you do. It is important for you to understand that not everyone has the same things at stake if a mistake is made. You must understand what is truly driving these individuals to do the right things and make good decisions. This gives you some insight as to how they will react in the heat of the moment. If their drive comes from something with substance such as family, the team, or religion, they are more likely to stand firm in the heat and make good rational decisions. If they are only driven by shallow things such as money and fame, they will probably fold under pressure and make bad choices.

With the right people around, you are not guaranteed to make all the right choices and decisions. It will, for the most part, help to keep you out of situations that are detrimental to your future. You most likely will not hang out in bad areas or in places that are dangerous if the other members of your crew have no interest in being there. You will not get caught up in things like drugs and gambling if the people you are with on a daily basis have no interest in those things. You can avoid or responsibly handle hostile situations such as fights and confrontations if you are not with hot headed individuals who are looking for conflict.

∞

Travis

Growing up on the south side of Chicago hostility was hard to avoid. In elementary school, I got into numerous fights because of my temper and not knowing how to walk away from confrontation. As I began to get older and mature, I started to realize that this was a weakness of mine, and that I need to make some adjustments before I ended up in a situation that would ruin my life for good. It was tough to admit that I was the problem, but I had to humble myself and figure out what needed to be done in order to protect my future.

I started to really pay close attention and evaluate the people I hung out with. It turned out that everyone I hung out with had this same weakness I did. Whenever we were faced with confrontation, none of us were strong enough to back away. In order to compensate for my weakness, I knew I needed to change my group of friends and surround myself with stronger, more grounded people. It was tough to walk away from guys that I had so much history with, but I knew it was for the better.

This was right around the time my mother decided to move our family to Michigan, so I was able to part ways without leaving any hard feelings, and I knew what traits to look for in my next crew. The group of friends that I grew up with in high school had a pretty good balance of tempers. Calvin and I were probably the most hostile of the bunch, but our other friends Duane, Ronnie, and Marshall knew how to keep us levelheaded. Being around these guys on a regular basis changed my temperament level completely. By the time I got to Michigan State, my temper was no longer an issue. I was then able to use what I had learned and be a support system for my new teammates and friends.

It is crucial that you understand your weaknesses and cater to them when selecting your group of friends. No one is going to be perfect, and you will all have your individual issues. As long as you guys can compensate for each other's weaknesses, you will be able to help each other make good decisions about how you spend your time. The environment you create around yourself plays a vital role in ensuring a successful future.

Travis B. Key & Ashton Henderson

HANDLING ADVERSITY

The only thing that overcomes hard luck is hard work.
— Harry Golden

Facing adversity is something that is inevitable in life. There are many tests and trials waiting ahead of you as you transition from a high school student-athlete to a collegiate student-athlete, from a teenager into adulthood. When you are working to achieve something great, there will be many challenges to overcome. If the road was smooth without any bumps or potholes, everyone would be traveling down it with you. The key to overcoming adversity is to not be naive about that fact that you will have to face it and to learn to embrace it as it comes your way.

Having this mindset will keep you focused and allow you to work hard to prepare yourself to overcome anything that is put in front of you. When you don't know exactly what is coming next, you should work extremely hard to be ready for the worst case scenario. You have no idea how many hits you will take the next time you are on the field, but you know that they are coming. The fact that you know the hits are coming should drive you to go hard and push yourself to the max during training so that your body is ready for the battle. When you are studying for an upcoming exam, you never really know exactly what questions will be asked by your teacher. So you prepare by making sure you understand all the material in the chapter and set yourself up for success.

Being able to handle adversity effectively starts with your state of mind and a healthy and strong spirit. You have to be mentally strong at all times. Your body will tell you to quit, and that it can't function anymore, but you must remember that your mind controls what your body does. Your heart may be broken, and depression may try to set in at times, but you have to remember that you have the ability to control those feelings and emotions. With a strong and positive state of mind, you have complete control over how you respond in any scenario.

You may have to face the reality of redshirting one day. Whether you are redshirted due to an injury or to give you more time to develop as a student-athlete, you must be positive about the entire situation. The purpose of redshirting is to ensure that you are mentally and physically prepared to face the challenges that lie ahead.

There will be times when you find yourself struggling academically and in need of a miracle to pass a class. You can't get so caught up in the struggles that you leave no time to find a solution. Having a healthy and strong spirit plays a huge role in how things work out for you.

Having an optimistic and energetic outlook in life will help you focus on the benefits and lessons to be learned from your tough situation as opposed to only seeing the negatives. You will naturally be more calm and collected when facing adversity, limiting the amount of stress that you put on yourself. This breeds self-confidence, which gives you the energy and drive to fight through the tough time.

On October 21, 2006, the Michigan State Spartans faced the Northwestern Wildcats in a football game on Ryan Field in Evanston, IL. This game would prove to be a picture perfect example of how to handle adversity and overcome a tough situation. To date, this game stands as the greatest comeback in NCAA Division I football history. The Spartans rallied to a 41–38 victory by scoring 38 unanswered points in the final twenty-two minutes of the game.

The Spartans started the game with confidence as they marched the opening drive down the field sixty-six yards. The Wildcats were able to stand strong and hold the Spartans to only a field goal on that drive. The next twenty-five minutes of the game were dominated by the Wildcats. It all started with a five-yard touchdown pass to finish the first quarter followed by a two-yard touchdown run on their first drive of the second quarter. The Wildcats were firing on all cylinders and followed up with a thirty-yard field goal and an eighteen-yard touchdown pass on their next two drives. The Spartans would go into halftime down to 24–3.

It didn't seem as if John L. Smith had motivated his troops at all with his halftime speech. The Wildcats took the opening kickoff and marched eighty yards down the field for a score in just five plays. The Spartans took the field for their first drive of the second half only to turn the ball back over to the Wildcats by throwing an interception on the first play. Two plays later, the Wildcats hit on a five-yard touchdown pass and what ended up being their last score of the game.

It turned out that Coach Smith's message to his Spartan troops about perseverance and playing for one another just took a little time to set in! The magic began to happen when the Spartans marched down sixty-five yards and connected on an eighteen-yard touchdown pass with nine minutes and thirty-six seconds left on the clock in the third quarter. The Spartan defense fed off this momentum and held the Wildcats to a three and out on the next drive. Eight plays later, the Spartans rushed in for another score capping off a fifty-three-yard drive. The Wildcats were beginning to feel the pressure and dug deep to spring a sixty-four-yard run on the second play of the ensuing drive. With the Wildcats knocking at the door, the Spartans answered with a huge defensive stop. Kaleb Thornhill intercepted a pass in the end zone to pull the momentum back in the Spartans favor.

With no scores added by either team on the next two drives, the next big play would come from the Spartan's special teams unit. On fourth down with the Wildcats preparing to punt the football, the Spartans charged through the line in an all- out blitz and blocked the punt. Ashton Henderson scooped the ball up in the first big play of his career and scatted thirty-three yards for a touchdown. The Spartan defense would stand strong once again, forcing another three and out from the Wildcats on the next drive. The high-powered Spartan offense, full of confidence, marched the ball right back down the field sixty yards and rushed in for another touchdown from sixteen yards out. The momentum had officially changed. With five minutes and fifty-nine seconds left in the game, the scoreboard read Northwestern 38 Michigan State 31.

With all guns blazing, the Spartan defense would force yet another three and out on the next drive! At this point, there was not one person in Ryan Field who didn't think the Spartans were going to win this game! The Spartan offense took over and six plays later threw for a nine-yard touchdown pass to tie the game at 38–38. The Wildcats got the ball back with three minutes and thirty-two seconds left in the game. They were clearly rattled by the events that had taken place. They had absolutely blown a thirty-five-point lead in a little over a quarter of play. The

Spartan defense took the field, smelling blood in the water.

On the first play of the drive, the Wildcats dropped back for a pass and threw the ball deep down the middle of the field. Out of nowhere, Travis Key jumped the play and made the biggest play of his career at that point coming down with an interception. This would prove to be the final nail in the coffin for the Wildcats! After milking the clock as much as possible, the Spartans chipped in the game winning field goal from twenty-eight yards out!

The testament behind the story of Michigan State's historic victory was told in Mr. Harry Golden's quote on the first line of this chapter- The only thing that overcomes hard luck is hard work.

You can't overcome anything in life, no matter what it is, unless you are willing to put in hours upon hours of hard work to prepare yourself in advance. You have to be mentally and physically tough in the heat of the moment. The battle is not won while you are in the fire; it is won long before the first match is struck.

When things are going well for you during your collegiate football experience, it's easy to remain in good spirits as well as maintain a positive attitude. Keeping that positive attitude at all times is the challenge. Facing trials such as losing your starting position, the death of a loved one, the pressure of family, and other personal issues will test who you are!

Ashton

I believe that true character is defined when your back is against the wall, and you have to make difficult decisions to help better yourself as a person. Adversity creates an environment for you that is very uncomfortable, but in those trying times you must embrace this challenge in your life to make you stronger.

There may come a time in your collegiate football career when you are not playing up to your potential, and it just seems like every time you hit the gridiron you are not getting better. You feel like you are truly giving it your all but you are just at a stalemate. Many coaches make their assessment of your performance on a week-to-week basis. When you are not performing, coaches tend to look at the depth chart to see who's next in line to provide a spark to the team!

Ashton

When I was in a slump, it always seemed as though the next man behind me was making plays and was hungry to take my spot. I can assure you that there will be a time in your career when the depth chart is placed on the projector screen, and you are not with the starting group. In that moment, you have three choices: complain about it, take the initiative to get your spot back, or throw in the towel.

The goal of the coaches should be to put the best eleven men on the field at once, and if you are not producing, you will get replaced instantly. Adversity tends to strike when you least expect it, and it often happens at a time when things are going well for you. It's hard to bring the same enthusiasm and energy to practice each day after you have lost your starting position.

You must be a team player first and foremost and keep a positive attitude. You then have to evaluate yourself and figure out what it is that you need to do individually so that you can earn your spot back. Collegiate football is a business, and coaches can't afford to place guys who are not producing on the gridiron. You are encouraged to never get complacent in anything that you do because you will lose out on so many things in life.

Ashton

The game of football has taught me many valuable life lessons that have helped me in my own personal life. There were times when I wanted to quit, but I constantly remind myself of what my teammates and I achieved in Evanston, Illinois against Northwestern! That day gave me the foresight to know that I can overcome any obstacle in my life if I just continue to persevere.

Another example of an adverse situation is dealing with death and family illnesses during the season. The death of a loved one is something that can be completely out of our control. All we can do is hope and pray that our family members and close friends are being protected.

Travis

Losing someone that you love dearly is a painful experience. On July 18, 2007, my sister Regina passed away at the age of thirty-two. It was completely unexpected and was one of the most devastating experiences of my life. She was a major part of my foundation and has been instrumental in helping me achieve the things that I have achieved.

The timing of losing a loved one is never good, but I had a lot on my plate at the time, and this made my load seem unbearable. I was in the process of trying to earn my scholarship back from a Coach Mark Dantonio and the new coaching staff. I was also in the midst of a very competitive position battle and wasn't even sure if I was going to come back for a fifth year at Michigan State. My situation was heated, and losing my sister made it even worse.

I decided to take a step back and evaluate my life, the people in my life, and the direction that my life was headed to. In doing so, I realized how important it was to my sister to see me not only finish college but complete my dream of playing collegiate football. She was there to pick me up and push me through the tough times and challenges I faced as a walk-on. There were many times when I wanted to quit, and she was there to encourage me, giving me the drive to keep pressing on. I realized that I would be letting her down if I decided to throw in the towel and not finish my last season of eligibility.

The event of losing Regina turned from being a life-shattering event to my main motivation as I vaulted through my senior season. I knew that I had control over how I was going to respond in that situation. Focusing on honoring my sister's name helped me persevere. I wore her name on my wristband every single football game that I played in after she passed away as a reminder to keep grinding no matter how tough the situation seemed.

∞

Being a part of a team is very special especially when you have one hundred plus other guys who care for you like a brother. This game we call life is not made to be taken for granted at all. We have to embrace the challenging times, so we can be an inspiration to someone else who will face the same issues.

Adversity will come in many different shapes and forms. We have to mature and take on the challenges that are presented. Whether it's dealing with a position loss, death, or family illness we have to be strong and courageous in order to make the best out of our situations. Handling adverse situations will build strong character and help you face the bumps and potholes of life when your days on the gridiron have been exhausted.

SWAGGER/CONFIDENCE

The Urban Dictionary defines the word Swagger as "How one presents him or herself to the world. Swagger is shown from how the person handles a situation." Swag is all about how confident you are in your skills to do whatever it is you do!

This confidence is built as a result of great preparation. Just showing up on campus and claiming that you have swagger won't cut it! If you don't put in the work before you get there, you will just be another perpetrator and will eventually be exposed. The guys who come in talking the most before they even hit the field, we call them "jaw jackers," are usually the perps! Your swagger will speak for itself if it exists. Don't act arrogant and rebel. Just be confident in your ability.

Travis

This concept reminds me of a quote by one of the most successful people of our generation, Will

Smith. In an interview on the Today Show, Will explained that "The separation of talent and skill is one of the greatest misunderstood concepts for people who are trying to excel. Talent you have naturally. Skill is only developed by hours and hours and hours of beating on your craft!"

Let's compare swagger to another one of the most successful hip-hop artists in the business today, Clifford Harris (better known by his stage name T.I.). Often you will find many artists trying to emulate his style. It's most likely because of the level of swagger he projects. T.I. is known for being one of the most dedicated and hardworking individuals in the studio and behind the scenes. When it's time for him to perform, his confidence level is through the roof, and he has an aura about himself that is hard to match. He has mastered his craft by putting in the hours of preparation. This ideology of swagger has been around for quite some time and has transcended over time.

When talking about swagger, the University of Miami Hurricane football teams of the 80s and 90s comes to mind as well. These guys were relentless and really knew how to play football with swagger. America had never experienced to a bunch of guys who played with so much emotion and energy on every single snap. The "U," as all football fanatics around the country referred to them, took collegiate football by storm. Many people didn't understand or appreciate the fact that these guys trained and prepared extremely hard every single day in order to play with the energy and emotion they played with. Those misconceptions and the fact that they may have talked a little too much led to fans and the media labeling them as arrogant.

In the late 80s, the world was introduced to Deion "Primetime" Sanders who took the concept of swagger and created his own definition. Until Deion, no one had ever witnessed someone train in 14k gold jewelry and a fitted cap. He is the originator of the concept "when you look good, you play good!" This mindset allowed Deion to play with great confidence and become the greatest defensive back to ever play the game. We have taken this type of swagger to new heights in the twenty-first century with Nike pro combat jerseys, gloves, cleats, and many other accessories that you put on.

There will be many days when you start to question your ability and truly ask yourself: am I really supposed to be here? It does not matter what level of collegiate football you play; somebody will be bigger, stronger, and faster than you. You cannot be afraid to make a mistake or to get beat by a veteran. Many coaches are looking for guys who are willing to compete each and every day. You are going to make mistakes, and when you do make them, go full speed. You must remain confident at all times, and trust your ability no matter what you encounter.

Ashton

I can remember vividly my first time going against a veteran wide receiver during a pass skelly period. This guy was six feet and six inches tall plus two hundred forty pounds of pure muscle. He could run as swift as a gazelle. Immediately, I began to think, what have I gotten myself into, and how am I going to shut this guy down? As mentioned in the previous chapter, I had to rely on a tactic that would help me guard this guy. As a cornerback, the battle can be won or lost within the first five yards. I was able to utilize my technique to stick with this guy and really harass his route with my aggressive play. After that moment, my swagger was on an all-time high. I felt that I could cover any receiver who walked God's green earth. Due to my attention to detail, I was given the nickname "the technician" by my position coach, Harlon Barnett, as well as my teammates and it is something I am very proud of.

If you use proper technique on every play, it will provide you the chance to be successful. That is the mindset you must develop as you embark on this journey. You cannot be afraid of anyone! No matter how big or fast they are you have to compete!

Many people judge football players by labeling them arrogant people who think they are better or more deserving than others. This is due to years and years of players not knowing how to conduct themselves in a non-football environment. You have to carry yourself in a very humble and polite manner when you are away from the game. Remember, swagger is not about being loud and obnoxious but about being confident. It is possible to approach fans, professors, and even the young ladies on campus with great confidence while remaining respectful. The way you communicate and interact with people is a huge part of creating a positive brand for yourself and your team.

Maintaining your swagger will allow you to achieve some great things throughout your collegiate experience. You must embrace the challenges that will be presented to you and always be ready to compete.

The Bible says in Colossians 3:23 (NIV), "Whatever you do, work at it with all of your heart, as working for the Lord, not for human masters." This simply means give a hundred percent in whatever you are doing. You should not focus on trying to impress the coaches but on giving your best effort in everything you do. You have been blessed with a God-given talent, and effort is one of the only things in life that he has given us one hundred percent control of. Remember, Swagger can only be developed through confidence that is built on a foundation of hard work!

HOMESICKNESS

Ashton

Any change in life opens the door to the possibility of missing the past. For many student-athletes going off to college is the first time they will be away from home for an extended period of time. The distance between home and the university you attend plays a large role in the emotions you will feel. Many student-athletes know they don't want to be more than a few hours from home, others are comfortable with a day's drive, while some go away knowing they will have to adjust to only being able to return home on a flight.

Collegiate athletics makes this situation a little more unique. While some students have the freedom and schedule to be able to easily travel on the weekends, student-athletes are commonly faced with a less flexible situation, especially during the season. You will also want to consider travel expenses for your parents, family, and friends to visit and watch you play. Do they have the resources to be present as often as you or they would like? Everyone's situation will be different, but having gone through the experience and emotions, I can try to offer some suggestions to help homesickness.

I was someone who chose to accept that I would only be able to return home on flights. I can remember preparing to leave Tallahassee, Florida for East Lansing, Michigan like it was yesterday. This was a very trying time for my family and I due to difficult situations that were on the horizon. My mother was very emotional about the fact that her youngest child was leaving the nest, as well as my father being very ill at the time, and my older brother moving away to start his new job in Atlanta with Nappy Boy Entertainment.

My father's situation made it very hard for me to leave home because I did not know if this would be the last time we would be together. I was concerned about leaving my mother behind to deal with taking on the challenge of taking care of him on her own. My father was actually in the hospital during the time I was preparing to leave for school. Due to his condition, the doctors mandated that he remain in the hospital until he gained his full strength. I knew my parents wanted me to attend school and not worry about things back home, so I had to trust that everything and everyone would be taken care of.

I truly admire my mother for the way she handled the situation at the time. I know things were very tough for her, but she seemed to always be in good spirits. My mother is my hero, and I am glad that God was able to provide her with the strength to deal with these issues. As soon as we arrived at MSU, the excitement of this new chapter in my life took over; but deep down inside, I knew I would truly miss my family.

After a very long week and the conclusion of parent orientation, my mother and I decided to treat ourselves to dinner at Red Lobster. We knew that we would not see each other for another three months when football season began, so we thoroughly enjoyed our time together before she went back to Florida. Everything seemed to be going well at dinner until I looked away for a split second and turned back to see my mother in tears. Immediately, I dropped my fork to console her and assure everything would be all right. My mother finally experienced a breakdown and all her emotions took over at once. I honestly was speechless.

After my mother's tears began to fade away, a family that was dining next to us came over to check on my mother. The Roberts Family approached us to make sure we were ok and to offer a lending hand of support. My mother explained to them that she was dropping me off at school, and she was concerned that I did not have family members in the Michigan area to look after me. The Roberts Family said, "Don't you worry, Mrs. Henderson, Ashton will be fine." My mother's million-dollar smile found its way back on her face as they talked and exchanged phone numbers, and this made my mom feel a lot better about leaving me in Michigan.

The Roberts Family became a part of my extended family at MSU. They kept in touch with me all through undergraduate and even during my journey through graduate school. They called me at least twice a month to make sure I was doing well and also invited me to attend church with them. This is how I knew that Michigan State University was the right place for me. My parents were very leery about me attending school up north, but after our encounter with the Roberts Family, my mother was certain that MSU was the place for me as well.

I was also able to link up with my middle school basketball coach who, soon after I began school, relocated back to his hometown in Michigan. Although he is a Michigan fan, he took a Spartan under his wing to make sure that I had a support system around me. I cannot thank Coach Henderson and his family enough for all they did for me while I was in Michigan. This was just the beginning of many lifelong friendships that were on the verge of being formed while I was in school.

As time passed, I really started to get homesick and did not know if I was going to make it. I can vividly remember being in my dorm room staring at the walls and just wishing that I could go back to Florida. College was starting to not seem so appealing after all. East Lansing is pretty quiet during the summers, and no one is on campus but football and basketball players and a few other students. This only made matters worse because there were no social events going on to get my mind off things that were occurring back home. I was constantly thinking about my father and many other issues that transpired since I had left. Not to mention, I was trying to maintain a healthy long distance relationship with my high school sweetheart.

As time progressed, I started to bond with the other freshman football players who were in my recruiting class. We were such a diverse group of guys from various places such as Canada, Kentucky, Florida, Pennsylvania, Ohio, New York, and a few other countries and states. One of the best discussions we would always have was about what state has the best high school football! We would literally debate this topic for hours just to make sure we represented for our states. However, even though we would have these debates, everyone knew that Florida has the best high school football in America! Having my new teammates around made my transition a lot smoother because we were all dealing with the same issues.

These new relationships helped me get over being homesick. Being away from home is tough, but it's a part of becoming a man and seeing what life has to offer you. This experience really helped shape me into the man that I am today and taught me how to stand on my own two feet. Months after my arrival, I hated Michigan and wanted to go home! After opening up a little, the homesickness continued to fade overtime. As the old saying goes, "Time flies when you are having fun."

My freshmen summer was a blur as our team geared up for the upcoming season. The most exciting part for me was that I knew I would see my family soon! My father was doing much better and was back at home from the hospital. This gave me one less thing to stress about while I was on campus.

Some things will transpire while you are away at school such as illness, deaths, and many other things that can affect you. Do not be afraid to seek help from the counseling center and many other resources that will be offered to you on campus. These issues can affect your performance in the classroom and on the gridiron. Surrounding yourself with positive people that you are comfortable discussing such issues with is a huge part of making a smooth transition.

My parents came to almost every home game in Spartan Stadium to support me. An important part of those Saturdays for my parents were the Spartan football tailgates. Before and after every home game, our parents would grill and just hang out for hours. This gave them the opportunity to engage with players as well as get to know the other parents on a more personal level. My parents loved to attend the tailgates and especially hangout with the Wiley and Weaver families.

The Wiley and Weaver families, being from Michigan, both treated me like a son and took care of me. They always made sure I had a place to go for the holidays whenever I was not able to make it home. They genuinely cared about my well-being and loved me as their own son. I am truly grateful to have them in my life. My parents are still close with those families, and it all started at the football family cookouts.

When you are choosing a college, you have to select a place where there is a family atmosphere. There were so many people who became a part of my extended family while I was at MSU. Gordon and Jane Spink played a vital role in my life while I was a Spartan especially after my playing days were over. I met Gordon at Discount Tire during my sophomore year when we both had flat tires. We had an opportunity to spark an interesting conversation about Spartan athletics, and he was able to make the connection that I played football for MSU.

Life is about building relationships, and I was very fortunate to be surrounded with good people who help me feel like Michigan was my home. Lanita Brown was someone else who came into my life once I reached campus. Mrs. Brown, also known as the Cookie Lady, makes the best chocolate chip cookies known to man and continues to bake her world famous cookies for the Spartan nation. Her role was the team grandmother, and everyone loved having her around because she was so pleasant. I could name so many people who treated me like I was their own while I was at Michigan State, but I would need to write several chapters on each person. These are the stories that you will have to share with your children about your collegiate experience one day. It's such a joy to remissness about good college memories and how you get to meet so many people and make lifelong relationships from all over the globe.

Another component that helped me get over my homesickness was being involved in Athletes in Action (AIA). AIA is a Christian sports organization and their motto is "Where God and sport unite!" I am not trying to offend anyone or persuade anyone's current beliefs, but I was brought up in a Christian *home, and I wanted to connect with other like-minded brothers in Christ while I was in Michigan.*

I was able to attend the weekly Bible study meetings on Tuesday nights with other athletes on campus. The meetings consisted of games, praise and worship, and many other things to help me strengthen my Christian walk while on campus. AIA gave me the support that I needed to maintain the course and also held me accountable for my actions. Phil and Julie Gillespie are truly impacting lives at Michigan State University through this wonderful organization. If this is something that interests you, I encourage you to get plugged in and ask your team chaplain about AIA, FCA, or Campus Crusade when you get on campus. AIA was a huge support to me, and it helped me get over my homesickness as well.

You may come from a different situation or a different environment, but homesickness will set in at some point in time during your transition into college. Especially if you are from a place where you cannot drive home on the weekends to see your family and close friends. I encourage you to go home with your roommate and get to know his family while you are in school. This will help you out tremendously and will also allow you to fill that void in your life. Do not get me wrong; there is nothing like your mother's or grandmother's home cooked meals, but having other people provide you meals and support you will serve you well in college.

STUDENT-ATHLETE DEVELOPMENT

Ashton

I had the privilege to serve as a graduate assistant for Angela Montie in Student-Athlete Support Services at MSU for two years. Angela has more than fifteen years of experience working with student-athletes on career preparation, resume prep, community service initiatives, award and honors. She also serves as the chairperson of the Student-Athlete Advisory Committee (SAAC). She is constantly cultivating relationships with companies to help student-athletes find jobs when their playing days are over. She genuinely cares about student-athletes and wants them to succeed in all of their future endeavors. Angela is also a former student- athlete, so her connection with us was really special because she could relate to everything we were facing.

To be completely honest with you, I walked by Angela's office multiple times my freshmen year and did not know what she did. I was too shy to investigate and ask her what her day-to-day job functions were. However, I asked a few of my teammates about her role, and they told me that I needed to meet her because she was a very resourceful person. I went to her office a few days later and introduced myself. Angela took the time to talk with me about everything that the Student-Athlete Development program had to offer me at MSU such as community service, personal development, career development, and many other things. I was truly amazed to hear about all these wonderful opportunities and I began to stop by her office more frequently.

As student-athlete development programs become more prevalent on college campuses, we want to encourage you guys to make sure that you take advantage of this great opportunity in your life. You will not be able to play football forever, so it's essential that you equip yourself with skills that will be transferable in the real world to help you succeed.

COMMUNITY SERVICE

There are many ways that you can serve your community while you are playing collegiate football such as volunteering at a local hospital, raising money for Teams for Toys, participating in March is Reading Month, and many other opportunities that will be available to you at the school that you attend. As a college athlete, you are given a platform to serve your community whether you accept it or not. You are automatically deemed a leader in the community whether you are a four-year starter or you only receive limited or no playing time. This is something that you just cannot shy away from because your community needs you.

However, no one is going to force you to participate in community service activities while you are in college. This has to be something that comes from inside. The desire to give back to your community and make a difference in someone's life has to be genuine. Each of us has someone in our lives who has made a significant impact or contribution. We have to keep this in mind while in college. Take time and make sure that you give back to brighten someone else's day.

∞

Ashton

While at MSU, I visited the children's hospital to hand out teddy bears and spend time with kids who were very ill. Some of the children had life-threatening diseases and other illnesses that caused them to be in pain all day. We went to visit several of the rooms, and I had never experienced so much joy from children who were on the verge of possibly dying. This truly changed my perspective on life and made my problems seem very small.

The children felt a connection with us because the university has strong ties to the community, and their day changed drastically for the better. I can guarantee you if you volunteer your time at your school, you will have the same impact on children in the community you serve as well as experience gratification to know you made a difference. I encourage you to make a difference while you attend college. It will truly make your collegiate football experience more enjoyable and will make you feel good about yourself.

PERSONAL DEVELOPMENT

Another essential component to your success in college is personal development. Personal development is an element of development that focuses on making sure the student-athlete develops skills to become a well-rounded individual. Some of the personal development activities consist of attending speaking engagements on campus, being a part of an organization, and just learning from others who are around you.

The university will have world-renowned speakers come to impart knowledge to students. This is something that we encourage you to be a part of while you are on campus. For example, President Barack Obama came to MSU before he was elected president to speak about issues that needed to be addressed in the 2008 election. This gave our student-body the opportunity to be informed and to know what was going on within our nation. This was a once in a lifetime opportunity to hear the president of the United States of America and engage in conversation with other students about the topics President Obama discussed.

Another essential piece to personal development is joining a campus organization. This is something that many student- athletes shy away from because it is time-consuming. We find it easy to make time for social events, girlfriends, and video games; but when it comes to joining something that can develop our skills as a person, we do not want to be a part of it. These opportunities will give you access to other young professionals who can help you gain experience. We encourage you guys to join a club that is of interest to you within your major to network with other like-minded professionals.

Ashton

This is something that I truly regret not taking advantage of while in college. I made excuses for myself and did not get serious about joining campus organizations until my junior year and was behind the curve. The time is now — when you arrive on campus, to be a part of something besides the football team. I loved being around my teammates, but sometimes you need an outlet to learn from other individuals on campus to make yourself better.

The last component of personal development is learning from others around you. Being a collegiate student-athlete, you can easily lose touch with the rest of the campus. You will be fortunate to have resources such as state of the art academic centers, free tutoring, and access to many other privileges that students on campus do not have. This creates an isolated environment. You are encouraged to interact and learn from other students in your classes and around campus. Taking advantage of the time you will have to get to know your professors and pick their brains is also key. These things will help your development as a person, allowing you to utilize skills learned from others around you.

CAREER DEVELOPMENT

It is vital that you take advantage of the opportunities you will have to prepare yourself for the real world as soon as possible. As freshmen, you need to identify what your interests are and create a career path that will lead you there. This may be an adjustment, but you will need to follow what you are passionate about and not what your parents want you to become. Often, kids rely on their parents for career direction and end up in a major they absolutely hate. Parents, please give your children an opportunity to explore what they like because it will surely make their collegiate football experience much better.

There are many resources on campus that offer resume preparation. You can get assistance with cover letters and take part in mock interviews to equip you with the confidence you will need throughout the interview process. Resume prep takes time and is a process. When you meet with someone on campus for the first time, your resume will most likely not be complete. Building a resume is like forming pottery. You have to continually shape and critique your resume in order to get it exactly where it needs to be. Starting the process early gives you a huge competitive advantage when it's time for your job search.

Attending career fairs while in college is highly encouraged. This gives you adequate practice on how to engage in professional conversations with companies. You will walk away understanding exactly what is looked for in new employees. Career fairs are the perfect platform to begin circulating your resumes as well. Many companies like to hire student-athletes because of our understanding of teamwork, our competitive nature, and the innate ability that we have to want to succeed in everything that we do.

Take time to find out where your school's campus career center is located and make a visit. This place is full of information, opportunity, and resources to help you transition from a student to a professional. You must be as serious about your academics as you are about football. Always keep in mind that you are only one play away from your football career ending. Please take your academics seriously, and make sure that you are setting yourself up for a future of success along the way. Seek counsel from individuals who you know are well-rounded and ask them to mentor you along the way. This will help you reach the goals that you have set for yourself academically and athletically.

NETWORKING

One of the greatest things you will be exposed to in college is the opportunity to network with people. Networking is one of the most powerful tools being used to get to know individuals who can enhance your career path. The old saying "It's not what you know but who you know" comes to mind when discussing this topic. This phrase deems to be true in so many facets of life, and you will fully understand its true meaning once you enter the real world. In college, it is important that you get a jump-start building your "who you know" list and take advantage of the opportunity to build a strong rapport with your professors, classmates, coaches, and teammates.

The relationships you build with your professors can serve to be a huge asset. Many people will argue that college classes are too big to get to know your professor on a first name basis. Those who support this argument lack the will needed to be successful in the course. If you take the initiative on the first day of class to introduce yourself, demonstrate hard work, participate, and be on time you will gain a tremendous amount of favor from your professors. That surely does not mean that you will receive "special treatment" because you are a student- athlete. You should abide by those principles because it's the right thing to do to gain respect from your professors. In fact, most professors already know who you are due to the weekly progress reports, attendance, and travel letters communicated between them and the academic support staff. Trust that your professors know exactly who you are and are just waiting for an opportunity to get to know you personally.

Many professors are well connected and are eager to help students who show they want to be helped. There will be many professors you should get to know because they can serve as a resource for you down the road. If you can't find the time to connect with them in person, don't be afraid to reach out to them via e-mail and set up an appointment to look at different careers within your particular area of study. You will be surprised who they know and how they can help you along the way. Also, keep in mind that once you connect with them, you are now a part of their network, and they will gladly endorse you for other opportunities.

Travis

I was able to take advantage of my time at MSU and build very sustainable relationships with quite a few of my professors. I always made it a point to have conversation with them before or after class and participate in discussions during class. I sat in the front row in every class to make sure they were able to put a face with my name. This extra effort made them feel appreciated and let them know I was engaged in the subject. Doing this made my professors want to go the extra mile for me and make sure I was on track to do well in their courses.

When it was time for me to hang up the cleats and pursue a career using my degree, I was able to reach back and lean on those same professors to help in my transition. Although it had been three years since I last communicated with any of them, every professor I contacted knew exactly who I was and was eager to help. I was able to get connected with people they knew in the industry, obtain inside information on available jobs, and receive great insight on what companies were looking for in candidates and what I needed to do to position myself well. I was able to land *five interviews with major companies within the first month of my search, and that all stemmed from having great rapport with my undergraduate professors.*

Another important networking opportunity you must take advantage of is the time you spend with classmates. These individuals can sometimes be the most resourceful people around you because you share common interests and goals. Being able to share ideas with each other and generate new concepts together creates a special bond.

Ashton

I had the opportunity to create a marketing campaign with several classmates to help the Michigan State Federal Credit Union keep MSU seniors from closing their bank accounts. At that time, I was not the best person with utilizing Adobe InDesign, but I was able to learn and actually enjoy these new experiences because I was learning a new craft that brought our group closer together along the way. This experience truly taught me how to network and learn from other individual's skill sets to enhance my abilities.

We each brought a different element to the group, and we all grew to learn each other's strengths and weaknesses very quickly. After months of planning, we put together a stellar marketing campaign called The Benefits of Staying Connected! We came up with an array of benefits on why seniors should keep their accounts. We did such a great job with the presentation that I convinced myself to keep my account when I relocated back to Florida.

This is something that I would have never done my freshman year because I was afraid to branch out and meet new people. As collegiate football players, it's very easy to isolate yourself from these experiences, but I am glad I was able to get over my fears. However, if I would have been driven to participate earlier in my career, I would have been more versed in many of the things I learned during this group project.

This time together will help you understand and shape your career path as well as identify those around you who have aspirations to head in the same direction. You, along with those individuals, will be the future of the industry you aim to be in. Therefore, your paths will most likely cross again. Having already built a relationship in college will only enhance the quality of business you are able to do together. A scenario that is more likely to occur is for one of your classmates to be employed at a company you aspire to work for. If you have a great relationship with that person and are a part of their network, chances are, they will do what they can to help you. Remember, "It's not what you know but who you know" that will land you the job.

The time you spend with your teammates is another networking tool you must capitalize on. It is important that you put forth effort to have conversation with teammates about each other's goals, interests, and areas of expertise. You will be amazed when you see how many resources you have, sitting right in your locker room that you never knew existed. You will find yourself connecting with teammates who can impact you immediately by helping with subjects you struggle in, giving advice on classes they already took, or simply connecting you with someone they know can help you.

This exercise will also serve as a future benefit as you and your teammates enter the professional world. A solid network is a two-way street. You will have knowledge of what your teammates are doing professionally if you are in need of an opportunity, and, on the other hand, be able to identify who is a good fit for a position you are trying to fill at your company. Don't just focus on the teammates you hang out with on a regular basis, but have conversations with the teammates you rarely cross paths with outside of football as well.

Ashton

Many of my teammates have left the gridiron to achieve some amazing things such as becoming lawyers and doctors, playing in the NFL, and pursuing entrepreneurship. I want to encourage you to keep in touch with your teammates and help each other obtain your dream jobs. I was fortunate to have teammates around me who had similar interests, which in turn helped us stay in touch even after our playing days were over.

Be a resource for one another. Always remember that each and every day in college is an interview process. If you are respectful, punctual, and humble, your professors, classmates, and teammates will want to help you out with anything you set out to do.

SOCIAL MEDIA

The emergence of social media has changed the way that we communicate and connect with people. Social media is the driving force that helps us stay connected with family and friends, and interact with people. There are many different social media outlets with millions of users, and the numbers continue to grow each day. Most college students frequently utilize these outlets to stay connected with the rest of the world and to socialize with different people.

These networks all have similar capabilities and student- athletes often forget that information shared on these sites are all displayed in real-time. This means that alumni, future employers, and opinion leaders will be able to view your page simply by searching your name. Many college recruiters are now constantly viewing prospective student-athletes pages to see what they are conversing about with their friends. Collegiate football coaches are not just looking for guys who are physically gifted anymore, they are looking for young men who embody character and integrity and will treat others with respect.

Many high profiled recruits have lost their scholarships to universities because of the inappropriate things they have displayed on social media websites. It's very important to understand that when you make your decision on what school you will attend, you not only represent yourself but that school as well. As a collegiate football player, you are now an ambassador for your school. This pressure can be overcome by considering who will be affected before you post things to the public. Sometimes you have to ask yourself, would my mother or grandmother approve me saying this? Would this tarnish my school's brand if I hit send? Asking these simple questions could be the difference between you losing your scholarship and getting the opportunity to live a dream.

Most schools are very good about making sure that student-athletes go through media training and teaching about how to effectively utilize social media when you arrive on campus. Some student-athletes don't listen and end up posting derogatory things that reflect on the team and the program. The moral of the story is to make good decisions about what you are sharing with the world and you will be fine. Social media outlets were created to unite people and create a unique community that draws people from all over the world together. It's a lot of fun to be a part of but be mindful of everyone that you represent now that you are a collegiate athlete. Coach Mark Dantonio would always say, "abuse brings control." This means if you do not utilize social media in a positive light, your privileges will be revoked.

There is another class of social media, professional networking, that we encourage all student-athletes to become heavily acquainted with. Sites such as LinkedIn are social media websites that help you connect with professionals in your field of interest. These websites can be thought of as an electronic resume that can be updated in real-time to share with others the great things you are doing professionally.

Ashton

Most people will argue that you really do not start getting serious about your career aspirations until your junior year, but I think the earlier you expose yourself with opportunities, the more prepared you will be for them. After your days on the gridiron are over, you will experience how competitive the real world really is, and it's important to utilize resources like LinkedIn to help you transition. I challenge you to come to college to be more than a football player. Make sure you take pride in your academics. Get involved with forums on LinkedIn and get to know people. It is important to build relationships with people who will advocate for you and tell employers that your experience as a student-athlete is transferrable to the workforce.

The characteristics that most student-athletes possess parallel what employers are looking for in their hires. Student-athletes are usually hardworking, disciplined, and perform well in high-pressure situations. Understanding how to effectively network through social media will create many opportunities for you down the road. If you continue to reach out and expand your network, creating the lifestyle that you want to have for yourself and your family will be much easier.

N.F.L. (NOT FOR LONG)

Many student-athletes begin dreaming about making it to "The League" at an early age but don't really understand what it takes to get there and have a sustainable career once you're there. Not only do you have to have an extremely high level of athletic ability, you must be able to beat the extreme odds working against you. The purpose of this chapter is not to discourage anyone's aspiration to make it to the National Football League but to provide insight on the realities and statistics surrounding ones chances.

We sat down with Kaleb Thornhill, Director of Player Engagement for the Miami Dolphins, to gain some insight on what student-athletes are up against when trying to make it to the National Football League. Prior to working for the Miami Dolphins, he received a bachelor's degree from Michigan State University while being a standout member of the football team. Immediately following his first degree, he went on to receive a master's degree from MSU as well.

Through this interview, we were able to understand valuable information that will help student-athletes position themselves to beat the odds! The information shared throughout this conversation will help you understand where your focus should be in order to assure yourself a successful future, whether it involves the National Football League or not.

BTG: What is your role in the NFL?

MR. THORNHILL: My role is Director of Player Engagement, engagement meaning prep, life, and next. My responsibility is to engage, educate, and empower individuals to reach their full potential in life.

BTG: Let's talk about your journey. What was your experience like as a student-athlete at MSU?

MR. THORNHILL: It was one big learning experience; the social education throughout your time in college is one of the most valuable lessons learned, really learning how to communicate with people and do it effectively. My overall experience was one big educational tool that provided me with the things I needed to be successful in life, or at least gave me a start.

If you want to talk about football, the experience was great. Obviously a lot is demanded from you. It is very hard to keep that academic and athletic balance. You have to stay focused because it is very easy to get distracted, especially in your earlier terms when you think that you are somehow bigger than the university because you play football!

BTG: What things did you value at the time? What was most important to you?

MR. THORNHILL: Looking back, I was lucky enough to have two parents who stressed education, so that remained very important. But at the same time, part of me was brainwashed to believe that football was to be the most valued. Just the pressures that you face from a national audience and being on TV every Saturday made me feel like that was my value. As I got older and learned and saw what was happening, I knew I needed to take advantage of my education, and I started to value it. That is when things changed for me, and I started to value relationships and building them.

BTG: Personally, where did your drive come from? What was your motivation?

MR. THORNHILL: I think for me, my motivation at the beginning was not to let down my family. Just to do my best in football and strive to be the best in that. I'm giving it to you from how I stepped in and how I came out of it. That drive for football never went away, but what I started to notice by my junior and senior year was that the drive came from something else.

I needed to start to define who I was as a person. What did I represent, and what did I want to be down the road? I don't think I fully answered that question until I was done playing football. I started to develop that in grad school. I go back to my defining sentence "to engage, educate, and empower." That is what drives me!

BTG: What was your road like getting to the NFL?

MR. THORNHILL: The road was not easy. I say this whole heartedly to everyone; never underestimate the power of a conversation. What happened for me was sending one e-mail that changed my life. One LinkedIn e-mail I sent opened the door for my opportunity in Detroit that changed my life.

It actually started back in college with Mark Hollis when I interned with him, before he was the athletic director. When he became the athletic director, I asked for a graduate assistant position in which I wanted to incorporate some player development principals and workshops to position myself for the exact role I am in today.

I went from that role to sending an e-mail to connect with Galen Duncan, who is the director of player development for the Detroit Lions. I didn't even know if there was a position open at the time, but one opened later for football operations and player development, and I applied for the opportunity. Lo and behold, Galen Duncan was the one conducting the interview along with Iain Nelson. I was fortunate enough to accept that opportunity when it was offered to me.

After my time in Detroit, there was a time when I didn't know where my life was going in terms of applying for jobs, and I didn't know if anything was open. I didn't have a clue what I was going to do. I knew I wanted to work as a director of player development, but at my youthful age, I didn't know if that opportunity would be offered to me. I decided to take one last shot at it, and I drove down to the NFL combine.

I didn't know if a job was open or not in Miami. I knew that the previous director had left, but I did not receive a call back from the GM when I reached out to him. So I chose to drive down to the combine not knowing if the job was open to seek him out and see if I could get an interview. After three days down there, I finally met up with the GM in the weight room and introduced myself. He told me that he had put that position on the backburner and hadn't thought much about it. He eventually went on to invite me to meet with him the following day. At that point, I didn't even have a shirt or a tie, so I called my mother up and asked her if I could borrow some money to buy a shirt and tie.

The next day, I interviewed with him. Everything was going well, but his biggest question was my youthfulness. I just told him about my experience in Detroit and how I gained the veterans' approval by simply being trustworthy, open, and honest. I then met with the Head Coach Tony Soprano and discussed the same things. They sent me on my way and told me they would be in contact, which they did three days later. They flew me down for a second interview and offered me the job that day, which I immediately accepted. Four days later, I was being flown down to Miami to become the director of player development.

BTG: What captivated you about landing the role that you have? What impact do or did you want to make?

MR. THORNHILL: Everything. I just thought about the opportunity to impact these young men beyond the game of football! To be able to meet with the rookies and be a guide in their lives beyond the game of football, getting those experiences and internships, job shadows, helping them continue their education and do what it takes to be successful in this world. What motivated me was that I could have a huge impact on these guys' lives on a daily basis.

BTG: How prepared are the players for life after football when they come in?

MR. THORNHILL: Not prepared at all. A lot of players may think they know what they want to do, or they say they want to do something; but if you ask them have they experienced it, they probably have not. That's not preparation. It's not always the player's fault. When you look at college and you are not able to conduct internships because of what is demanded from the athletes, it's not always their fault that the access was not there for them.

BTG: What do you feel should be done at the collegiate level to help better prepare them?

MR. THORNHILL: They must build better awareness. From the moment the student-athlete walks in, getting them to understand the realities of making it to the NFL, giving them tools, and the proper development when they transition in. Hold classes for them to prepare them for what is expected. Just because they play football doesn't mean they are going to be successful. There are tools that individuals need that they are lacking throughout college. I think it would be extremely helpful if colleges implement a development program not only to advise these student-athletes on class but to advise them on life.

BTG: What are scouts using to evaluate potential NFL talent?

MR. THORNHILL: They are evaluating talent based on the question that can somebody be accountable and dependable. I think that is what they are looking for—somebody who can be driven by the game of football and committed. They are looking for a whole student-athlete, meaning someone who does things right day in and day out. Coming into the NFL is a grind, and they are looking for individuals who can be a professional in all areas of their life.

BTG: How many guys in the NFL have a college degree on average?

MR. THORNHILL: On average it's about 47–50 percent.

BTG: Does being better prepared for life after football translate to being a better football player? Longer NFL Career?

MR. THORNHILL: Yes! It is proven that players with their college degree, which means that they are better prepared, play longer, and they make more money along the span of their career. That is fact. You look at that and think if you know what you are doing and are making the correct steps to be prepared for life after football, that is one less thing you have to worry about while you are playing football. I think they understand what their goals are; they have a better outlook on life and really what they want to accomplish. It all translates into being a better football player.

BTG: What type of adverse situations do players face that they seem to be the least prepared for when they come in?

MR.THORNHILL: One hundred percent relationships! Family mostly. They are not prepared for all the people that are going to come into their lives, and they are not prepared to say no! That is something that needs to be taught, and we go over this in our meetings. Not only how do you say no but how do you say it in a way where somebody is not going to be turned off. And how do you say no to family members and still show them love, not losing that relationship. Second would be financial, which triggers all the problems from everywhere else around their life with relationships. People expect a lot from them.

BTG: What are some common down falls for players who don't make it? Why do they fail?

MR. THORNHILL: They fail to prepare. They fail to answer the question that is tough to answer. Who am I beyond the game of football? If you can address that question or at least began to make some deposits and build relationships beyond the game of football by participating in internships and finishing your degree, you're going to make your life ten times easier. They fail by not understanding the type of income that comes after this game and understanding that money doesn't create happiness. I think they fail to find their true passion as well. Those things combined describe the common downfalls and why they fail.

BTG: Based on your experiences, what would you say is the typical mindset of rookie players as they enter the NFL?

MR. THORNHILL: Very young! It is one of those things where they are walking into something that they think is the most glorious thing in the world, but they don't understand the obstacles they are going to have to overcome, to be successful in this business, especially long term. Understanding what it is going to take to turn what was a part-time job into a full time job and what does that even mean. I think that is the biggest thing for them to understand, what a professional is. Not a professional football player, what it means to be a professional period.

BTG: What areas do they lack knowledge in the most?

MR. THORNHILL: Mentally, the biggest thing they struggle with is financial, in terms of financial relationships. Like I said before, just understanding what it takes to be a professional.

Physically, I think they lack an understanding of what it takes to keep your body in shape at this level and how to kick it up a notch, which is part of being a professional. They lack skills to be successful beyond the game of football. Obviously, I don't expect them to know everything, but without having any financial education and coming upon a large sum of money and not having gone through what the normal American has gone through in terms working their way up and learning how to manage their money by the time they are thirty something, they are forced to do it at a very young age.

They lack the experience of really being able to sit down professionally with people and determine who should be the core group in their life to help them to succeed. Socially, being able to communicate effectively with teammates is not an easy thing to do at this level because everyday somebody is trying to take your job. Being able to be themselves and not so tense is hard for these guys as well.

BTG: What is the life span of an NFL player? Are players aware of this when they come in?

MR. THORNHILL: No, I don't think they are as aware as they need to be. The average is 3.3 years. You look at that number, and you are twenty-five by the time you are done playing. To understand that you will be doing something else for thirty years or the rest of your life is hard for them to deal with.

BTG: Do you think the chances of making it to the NFL will continue to decrease?

MR. THORNHILL: Yes, because it's not getting any bigger. They are not expanding the roster. The amount of people who play football at earlier ages is increasing therefore the chances will continue to decrease.

BTG: How beneficial would it be for the NCAA to spearhead a player development initiative for student- athletes in college?

MR. THORNHILL: I can't even describe or put it into words how beneficial it would be. I think it would benefit every athlete. I think by implementing something where you can engage the athlete, educate, and empower them to be successful in life is positive. It is not only positive for the athlete; it's positive for recruiting. It is a tool that all of us need. Even the average college student will need this.

I think many students are lacking networking skills, relationship building skills, and really just the understanding that they are going to need help at some point. Understanding how to do those things and being taught how to do those things is extremely important. Providing these SAs with job shadows, internships, and opportunities to understand what graduate degrees are out there and what type of access they could possibly have would only increase by hiring a position in player development at a college level.

It is needed. Every NFL team has one; therefore, there is no reason every college student-athlete shouldn't simply because of the number of players that will not make it to the NFL. We are talking about 98 percent of players who will not be playing in the NFL. You want to affect those. You want to be able to impact the greatest amount. Why not invest in that. Like I said, it would help extremely in recruiting. It is a win-win situation all the way around.

Money Management

The lack of financial education has caused many setbacks and failures in the lives of college student-athletes. Not understanding how to set and follow a budget can lead to poor financial decisions that will hinder you in the short term and cause major damage to your future. Sporting News reported that 86 percent of college student-athletes live below the poverty line. This means you most likely won't have a lot of extra money to spend as a college student-athlete, even if you're on a full ride scholarship. It is crucial that you learn how to spend the money you do have wisely early on in your career!

Even though colleges and universities are beginning to understand the importance of providing mandatory financially education courses for student-athletes, we still have a long way to go before the tide will completely turn. Mississippi State University is spearheading this initiative by requiring their student-athletes to take a money management course during their first year on campus. Hopefully other universities will implement similar programs, but as of now it is up to you to take ownership of your short and long term financial health and position yourself for financial success.

Below you will find four valuable lessons about money we have learned over the years that we wish we knew going into college. We hope these will help you avoid some of the mistakes we have made or watched our teammates make!

1. Establish a budget and stick to it! Sit down with your financial aid advisor and make sure you understand how much money you have coming in and when that money will be available to you. Map out all of the expenses you have, not covered by your scholarship, and put a value towards each item. Be sure to include money for your social life as this will help you control what you spend in that area. This is where most over spending occurs.

2. Avoid the credit card trap! Many student-athletes get caught up trying to live above their means and accumulate thousands and thousands of dollars in credit card debt. Having a credit card can be a good thing as it is an easy way for you to build your credit score, but it must be managed

closely. Only spend what you know you can pay off at the end of the month. Only use your credit card to pay for things that are already in your budget.

3. Do not gamble! Many of you will be tempted to gamble with teammates or other students thinking you can win extra money to cover your gaps. You will be enticed to gamble on everything from video games to card games and shooting jump shots to shooting pool. This is the wrong solution! The fact that you have made it to this level of play indicates that you are a highly completive individual. Highly competitive people are the most vulnerable when it comes to losing control of themselves while gambling. In the end you always lose. It might be money. It might be trust. It might be friendships. Whatever it is, I promise you will lose something!

4. It is essential that you get in the habit of saving while you are in college. You may not have much to put away at the time, but every little bit adds up down the road. After determining what your budget is for

fixed expenses, we recommend that you consider how much you should save before allocating money for social activities. This takes discipline, but if you approach it the right way, you can position yourself to have a hefty down payment for a car or house when you graduate from college! At the very least you will have a reserve for any emergency situation that arise. Visiting a local bank or university credit union to open a checking and savings account should be one of the first thing you do when arrive on campus. Make this a priority!

On the next page you will find a budget template that will help get you started on the right track. It is important that you understand the exact dates you will receive your income and plan to reestablish your budget every 30 days.

College Student Budget

Financial Aid & Income

	Actual	Expected	Difference
Financial Aid			
Job			
Other			

Expenses & Accountabilities

Tuition			
Fees			
Housing			
Food			
Health			
Phone			
Car/Bus			
Gas			
Insurance			
Savings			
Social			
Other			

WHY WE WEAR THE JERSEY

Have you ever taken the time to understand the real reason athletes wear jerseys? Is it so we can be identified by the referees in a game? Is it so fans in the stands can tell what team we play for? Is it so our teammates can identify with us? Or does it have a deeper purpose?

Travis

As I sit and stare at the green and white No. 13 jersey that hangs on my wall, it is crystal clear to me the true purpose for the football jersey. On the front I see the words "Michigan State" elegantly stitched across the chest. On the back, I see my last name polished across the top. On the chest, back and two shoulders, I see large bright No. 13s boldly popping off the aggressive dark green background. To me, the jersey represents everything and everyone I was accountable to as a student-athlete.

∞

The words across your chest signify the responsibility you have to your school. You are accountable to uphold your commitment to being an intelligent student who uses good judgment in all of your actions – both inside and outside of the classroom.

The color of your jersey represents your current teammates and the past players who have worn the jersey before you. A legacy was created by those from the past, and your teammates are the ones sweating and bleeding with you every day to make sure everyone upholds that legacy and achieves success on and off the field.

The jersey number stands for the accountability you have toward yourself. You are accountable to grind and never give up in the face of adversity because of all of the hard work and sacrifices you made to prepare yourself for life.

The name on the back of your jersey represents your family and friends. These are the people who have invested in you, broken down barriers for you and pushed you to get better each and every day. You represent everything your family name is built on and are accountable to maintain a high level of honor and dignity around it. You owe it to them to be fully committed to giving your very best at all times.

Your jersey symbolizes accountability. It's not just about you. Being a student-athlete comes with responsibility and duty. Every time you put on that jersey, remember what it truly means and who it stands for. Give everything you have and make those you represent proud.

THE GOAL LINE

Ashton

One of my favorite verses is found in I Corinthians chapter 13:11 (NIV). It states, "When I was a child, I talked like a child, I thought like a child, I reasoned like a child. When I became a man, I put the ways of childhood behind me." This verse speaks to my development and growth stages while I was in college as well as the life lessons I learned to transition into a man. I came to East Lansing when I was eighteen years old, but I was supposed to be at the age you considered yourself an adult. However, I still had a lot of growing up to do because I was someone who depended on my parents and now had to figure things out on my own in college. I did not have anyone in my ear about coming home before midnight, encouraging me to study, and etc. These were things that I had to figure out on my own in order to be successful.

For example, it was storming outside, and I woke up around 5:30 AM because I could not sleep due to the tree branches scratching my dorm room window in McDonald Hall. So I did what any eighteen-year-old would do at that time, which is go back to sleep. This was one of the worst decisions I made because I had to wake up at 6 AM to ride my bike to the workout facility. I forgot to set my alarm, and I was going to be at least thirty to forty-five minutes late to my first collegiate workout. Unfortunately, my suitemate forgot to set his alarm also, so we both scrambled to get out of the dorm. We got dressed very quickly and began to ride our bikes as fast as we could. By this time, the storm had calmed down, and the sun was shining very brightly.

My teammate and I made to the facility, and we were pacing back and forth in the locker room because we did not want to make a bad first impression. It was too late. We finally got the strength to go inside to the full defensive team workout, and Coach Mannie yelled across the indoor and said, "Get on the line!" Marcus and I were welcomed to our first collegiate workout with one hundred yard up downs while the upperclassmen, and our other frosh teammates laughed at us. I was completely embarrassed, and after a few rounds of up downs, Coach Mannie lets us join our new teammates. I was humiliated, and I wanted to just turn back the hands of time to reach over to set my alarm clock to avoid this moment of shame.

After the workout concluded, the strength coach who taught me so many valuable life lessons pulled us to the side and said, "It's the little things that get you beat." Being on time is something you can control, and it's important to be timely to class, tutorial appointments, and anything you do in life. At that time, what he was saying did not resonate with me because I was still in shock that we were late to our very first workout. But now that I am in the work force, I make sure I am at least five to ten minutes early for everything. Marcus and I also made it to a point to never be late for anything else, and I can honestly say that we were not. Something so simple that was tragic at that time has taught me a life lesson: be on time! I think most college athletes know the race against time, and it's in our DNA to be punctual.

There are so many valuable lessons I learned in college that helped me transform into the man I am today. I think the choices you make in college will follow you for the rest of your life. The reason I say that is because my parents used to tell me that everyone is not your friend. This saying deemed to be true in college also. There will be times when your teammates call you at 3 AM because they just got in to an altercation with some local guys at the bar. What will you do? You are aware that there will be situations that could jeopardize your teammate's future. Will you choose not to say anything to coaches and just let him throw his life away? These situations will arise, and part of becoming a man in college is to separate yourself from foolishness, to keep your eye on *the prize of getting your degree, and to give yourself the chance to be fortunate to play in the NFL one day. Trust me, nobody is perfect; and you will make mistakes, but do not keep making the same mistakes because those same mistakes will eventually be detrimental to your future.*

Playing collegiate football at whatever school you attend will take up four to five years of your life. I can guarantee you that. But making sure that you apply the principles that you have learned in this book will prepare for most of things that you will face in college. The reason I say most is because it's still up to you to choose the lifestyle that you want your family to have in ten to fifteen years. You control your own destiny, and if you work hard, you will be able to achieve anything you set your mind too. Be sure to utilize the resources you will have around you like the career center, student-athlete development programs, and community services. This will ensure you will become the most well rounded student- athlete you were called to be.

Also, please do not get discouraged if you do not make it to the NFL. All this means is that God has designed a plan for your life, and if you trust him you will reap the benefits of a very successful life. Trust me, I told my fifth grade teacher that she will see me in the NFL one day, but unfortunately, that did not happen. However, I can assure you that I will be successful because my plans do not compare to what God has in store for me. Please do not think that I am trying to destroy your dreams, but I have witnessed former teammates who could not make the transition out of the game. You have to man up and have a plan B to provide for your family. I want the best for each and every one of you guys and that is why Travis and I set out to write this book. We also want each of you to strive for excellence not just on the field but also in the classroom.

Please utilize this book as a resource as you embark on the next chapter of your life. Collegiate football is waiting for you, and we are praying for your success and hope that you will make an immediate impact in the classroom, on the gridiron, and in the new community that you will be a part of. Make sure you leave a legacy at your school and achieve all your goals you set out to accomplish. When you leave the gridiron, make sure you leave a better man to help provide advice for the next frosh class who comes after you.

Travis

"Play until the whistle!"

This phrase has been pounded into our heads our entire athletic careers. No matter what sport you play, no matter what level you play at, all coaches preach this concept to their players. There is very good reasoning behind this. It teaches athletes to never give up on a play or repetition. It teaches athletes to give maximum effort every second they are preparing for or are in competition. It teaches athletes to always finish because anything can happen at any moment.

My faith, my family, and the experiences the game of football awarded me have molded me into the man that I am today.

He replied, "Because you have so little faith. Truly I tell you, if you have faith as small as a mustard seed, you can say to this mountain, 'Move from here to there,' and it will move. Nothing will be impossible for you."
Matthew 17:20 (NIV)

This verse has helped me form a solid foundation for my life. It has helped me to maintain the mindset that no matter what situations I face in my life, no matter how hot the fire gets, or how high the mountain is, I can sustain if I keep my faith. I owe my understanding of the power of God and the relationship I have with him to my sister Regina. She guided me to attend church at an early age and set an example on how to walk a Christian life.

The role my family has played in my life is immeasurable! From the unconditional love my mother gave, and the sacrifices she made for me, to the unconditional love I receive from my wife and children, and the sacrifices they make in order for me to live my dreams today – my family has always been my backbone. All that I do and all that I have ever done has always been for the benefit of my family and loved ones. They provide me strength when I am weak and encouragement when I am down. My goal in life is to make my mother proud of her son, my wife proud of her husband, and my children proud of their dad! My family is what drives me to achieve greatness. The way they feel about me at the end of the day is the measuring stick in my eyes!

I am fortunate to have played the game of football at every level. I have been blessed to learn and be mentored by some of the most intelligent men ever to coach in this sport. Football has been a tremendous part of molding me into the man I am today. It has taught me to be mentally and physically tough at all times. I have learned to know and be fully committed to the fact that I can overcome any obstacle I face if my head is on straight, I work hard, and I am properly prepared. It has taught me to persevere and to never give up on anything or anyone I commit myself to. It has taught me how to be disciplined and how to have structure in my life. It has taught me how to respect authority and realize there is always a lesson to be learned. It has taught me great lessons about leadership and about placing people along my path who demonstrate what the term truly means. And it has taught me the importance of establishing strong sustainable relationships with the people I choose to have in my life. Football doesn't define who I am, but it sure has helped me to understand the qualities a person should possess in order to live a high quality of life.

Athletics have so much to offer people. It is however a choice that each athlete must make whether to buy into the lessons being taught or not. We as athletes must learn to use these very important lessons and apply them to life after the game is done and over. When life gets tough and our family is depending on us to provide, we can never give up on them! We must maximize each day and give full effort in everything we do because nothing is guaranteed. We must cherish every moment we have with the people we love because every day and every second of our lives is irreplaceable. We must prepare for life's challenges with a reckless abandon so that we can be fit to hold the weight of those who depend on us when the time comes. We must always finish what we start and fight to the very end of our time because our breakthrough can come at any moment!

"Play until the whistle!" When we are in the moment and living the dream of being an athlete, it is hard to understand the power of the phrase. The earlier you realize the true message that is being delivered, the better off you will be in life. Football is a great game, and if you can embrace the experiences you have, grow in your faith, and develop a strong drive from the ones you love…You will be set to play long after the whistle is blown!

ABOUT THE AUTHORS

Ashton Henderson was born and raised in Tallahassee, Florida in a Christian home. From a very early age, his parents knew that God had a special calling on his life, but he had to trust him to do his will. Growing up in a middle class family, his parents worked extremely hard and made sacrifices to make sure he and his older brother, Antonio Henderson, had everything to be successful in life. His parents continued to sacrifice as they put him into private school to gain a great education and continue to strengthen his relationship with Christ along the way. He will always be indebted for their sacrifices because they nurtured and trained him to strive for excellence. They both taught their children what it means to be successful and not to make excuses when adverse situations arise in their lives. They showed them how to persevere and seek God for counsel and guidance through it all.

In the fall of 2006, Ashton was fortunate to choose Michigan State University over the University of Mississippi and UCLA to play Division I collegiate football. He was blessed to have a cornucopia of Division I offers and thoroughly enjoyed going through the recruiting process. He had a pretty successful career at Michigan State with notable starts against Michigan, Notre Dame, and Iowa just to name a few. He was named Defensive Attack Force Player of the week in 2007 for his performance against the Iowa Hawkeyes. MSU ended up losing in triple overtime, but it was one of his best performances in his career.

His most notable moment as a football player came early in his career. He was able to return a blocked punt for thirty-three yards to help fuel the greatest comeback in NCAA Division I football history during his freshman year. Many would argue that his touchdown helped provide the spark the team needed to get on track. MSU overcame a thirty-five point deficit, and that was the day Ashton realized anything in life was possible.

After earning his Advertising degree from Michigan State University in 2010, his playing days came to an end due to severely spraining his MCL during his senior season. He could not recover and get back to his potential to excel on the field. He was discouraged, devastated, and looking for the next challenge in his life.

He served as a graduate assistant in Student-Athlete Support services at Michigan State University and earned his master's degree in Public Relations. Ashton obtained a role as an Academic Program Specialist for football and the men's and women's track and field program at Florida State University before moving on to become the Associate Director of Football Academics at Clemson.

Currently, he has the opportunity to utilize his platform as an Associate Director of Football Academics |Seminole Leadership Program at Florida State University in Tallahassee, Florida and is happily married to Jasmyne. He also looking to continue his education by enrolling in the FSU MBA part-time to earn his MBA by 2019.

Travis Key was born in Harvey, Illinois—a south suburb of Chicago plagued with high drug, poverty, and crime rates. He and his older brother William were raised by his single mother,

Jacqueline, with the support of many family members, most notably their Grandmother Eva (Nana) and older sister Regina. Jackie often worked two or three jobs at once to make ends meet, which forced Travis to grow up at a very early age. Travis was frequently in trouble at school and at home. He began spending more time in the streets. His father, William Sr., was in his life but rarely under the same roof.

Living in such a negative environment and her boys not taking school as seriously as they should, Jackie made the courageous decision to relocate her family to Three Rivers, MI. Although Travis and William didn't understand it at the time, the decision was made to give them access to better opportunities as they entered high school. In high school, Travis became a standout student-athlete in football, basketball, and track, earning many academic and athletic accolades along the way. The move to Three Rivers not only gave Travis a new beginning, but it afforded him the opportunity to meet the love of his life, Giovanna, who would eventually become his wife.

In the fall of 2003, after turning down a few small school offers to play football, Travis decided to attend Michigan State University to pursue Engineering. Travis decided that he would walk on to the Spartan football team and earn himself a scholarship. Travis was given his shot to make the team at an open tryout in January of 2004 where he succeeded. The next two seasons, Travis earned playing time as a special team's player for the Spartans while earning Academic All- Big Ten honors in both years. By mid-season of his junior year, Travis had played his way into the starting line up as a safety for the Spartan defense.

After earning a Bachelor's degree in Packaging in May 2007, Travis decided to return to school for his last year of eligibility and pursue his master's degree. In the fall of 2007, he was selected as captain of the team by his teammates and coaches. This honor was a testament to all the hard work and leadership he displayed throughout his time in East Lansing. After a stellar senior year, he earned his fourth consecutive Academic All-Big Ten award and was selected honorable mention All-Big Ten as a player. He was rated one of the top safeties in the 2008 NFL draft class.

After facing the disappointment of not being drafted, Travis signed as an undrafted free agent with the Minnesota Vikings. He would go on to have a short two and a half year professional football career including stops in Cleveland, Detroit, San Diego, Indianapolis, and Montréal.

Travis retired from the game in the summer of 2010 and began his career as a packaging engineer. He received his master's degree in Packaging from Michigan State in the fall of 2012. Travis has five siblings Lillia, Regina, Damon, Latoya, and William. Travis currently works for the Kellogg Company and lives in Michigan with his wife, Giovanna, two daughters, Gianna and Malina, and son Matteo.